Eyes Wide Shut:
Re-Envisioning Christina Rossetti's Poetry and Prose

Melanie Ann Hanson

Melanie Ann Hanson

EYES WIDE SHUT:
RE-ENVISIONING CHRISTINA ROSSETTI'S
POETRY AND PROSE

ibidem-Verlag
Stuttgart

Bibliografische Information der Deutschen Nationalbibliothek
Die Deutsche Nationalbibliothek verzeichnet diese Publikation in der Deutschen Nationalbibliografie; detaillierte bibliografische Daten sind im Internet über http://dnb.d-nb.de abrufbar.

Bibliographic information published by the Deutsche Nationalbibliothek
Die Deutsche Nationalbibliothek lists this publication in the Deutsche Nationalbibliografie; detailed bibliographic data are available in the Internet at http://dnb.d-nb.de.

Cover picture: Dante Gabriel Rossetti. Portrait of the artist's sister Christina and mother Frances, 1877. Source: http://commons.wikimedia.org/wiki/File:Christinaandfrances.jpg. Public Domain.

∞

Gedruckt auf alterungsbeständigem, säurefreien Papier
Printed on acid-free paper

ISBN-13: 978-3-8382-0365-2

© *ibidem*-Verlag
Stuttgart 2012

Alle Rechte vorbehalten

Das Werk einschließlich aller seiner Teile ist urheberrechtlich geschützt. Jede Verwertung außerhalb der engen Grenzen des Urheberrechtsgesetzes ist ohne Zustimmung des Verlages unzulässig und strafbar. Dies gilt insbesondere für Vervielfältigungen, Übersetzungen, Mikroverfilmungen und elektronische Speicherformen sowie die Einspeicherung und Verarbeitung in elektronischen Systemen.

All rights reserved. No part of this publication may be reproduced, stored in or introduced into a retrieval system, or transmitted, in any form, or by any means (electronic, mechanical, photocopying, recording or otherwise) without the prior written permission of the publisher. Any person who does any unauthorized act in relation to this publication may be liable to criminal prosecution and civil claims for damages.

Printed in Germany

This book is dedicated to my incredible parents,
Florine and Milford Hanson,
who never ceased to amaze me and who never ceased to defend, support, and acknowledge me every minute of my life.

Contents

Acknowledgements 9

Introduction 11

1. "The Eye of the Mind" in Christina Rossetti's Poetry 21

2. Re-configuring Eve – Christina Rossetti's Reaction
   to John Milton's *Paradise Lost* in Rossetti's Poetry and Prose 47

3. What We Owe: Bankruptcy in Christina Rossetti's *Goblin Market* 77

Conclusion 103

Works Cited 105

ACKNOWLEDGEMENTS

The generosity and helpfulness of my editor in perfecting my text deserves kudos. Ibidem-Verlag has published my first two books, and their support and nurturing of my writing talents deserves an accolade. My appreciation goes out to the entire staff at Ibidem-Verlag for their dedication to their craft. I would be remiss if I did not mention that I first became interested in Christina Rossetti's beliefs and writings in a class I attended at UNLV in Las Vegas, Nevada taught by Dr. James Hazen. Hazen was the advisor on my master's thesis on Rossetti, and his dedication to the improvement of my writing and his inspiration as an instructor of English Victorian literature elicits my praise.

INTRODUCTION

My project is entitled *Eyes Wide Shut: Envisioning Christina Rossetti's Poetry and Prose*, because there is a connection between Stanley Kubrick's film and Christina Rossetti's writing, as improbable as that sounds. Stanley Kubrick adapted Arthur Schnitzler's *Traumnovelle* (or *Dream Story*) and directed the film version re-entitled *Eyes Wide Shut* in 1999. The film deals with dreams and fantasies, illusion and reality. People can think they see something clearly when they actually do not. Christina Rossetti's poetry and prose, written in 19th-century England, also deals with the concepts of what is real and what is not real, what is truth and what is imagined. She was intrigued by the human fixation on appearance (which she believed was vanity) that was mistakenly believed by lost souls to be what is true.

Her belief in the Tractarian precepts of the Oxford Movement, primarily expostulated by John Keble and John Newman, transformed Rossetti's outlook on perception. Her association with the Pre-Raphaelite Brotherhood also influenced her writings concerning what is real and what is not. The title of this book also speaks to the focus of the project, being the re-envisionment of Christina Rossetti's poetry and prose from three theoretical perspectives: deconstructionist theory, feminist literary theory, and Marxist literary criticism. The first chapter of this book explores Christina Rossetti's fascination with eyes and seeing. I believe that Rossetti was absorbed by Plato's "Eye of the Mind" and felt that the physical eyes must be shut so that the "eye of the mind" could be wide open. She connected the "eye of the mind" to her Tractarian religious beliefs. The mind's eye relates to Eastern religious philosophy as well in her writings. The mind's eye sees an alternate perception of reality.

There have been numerous critics in the past 15 years who have interrogated Rossetti's obsession with eyes and sight in her writings. I take these critics to task in the first chapter of this book where I discuss Rossetti's application of the theories presented in Plato's "The Allegory of the Cave" to her own writing. Rossetti uses the eye as a symbol of what is perceived applying Plato's "eye of the mind" to her theories based on her Tractarian faith, manifested in her poetry. Chapter two in this manuscript illustrates how Rossetti re-envisions John Milton's depiction of Eve in *Paradise Lost*. Although Rossetti was not a feminist, her re-working of the figure of Eve in her poetry and prose throughout her life speaks to contemporary feminist theory. Chapter two focuses on her poetic and prose writings although her prose writings that she completed near the end of her life are showcased in this chapter. The capitalist utopia is a fantasy world that Rossetti scrutinizes in her parable of power relations *Goblin Market*; this is the topic of Chapter three in this text.

My thinking on Rossetti, that has encompassed a 15-year pursuit of research, has been influenced by various writers. Michel Foucault's theory of the Panopticon (the gaze and the object of the gaze) and its subsequent re-application to feminist theory (primarily in the writings of Lorraine Janzen Kooistra, Pamela Banting, and Barbara Garlick) is of major importance to my discussion of Rossetti's fascination with eyes in her poetic and prose works discussed in Chapter 1 of this text. Diane D'Amico's discussion of Eve, Mary, and Mary Magdalence as a triptych gave rise to my thinking concerning Rossetti's reconstruction of Milton's Eve that is the focus of Chapter 2 in this book. Elizabeth Helsinger, Barbara Weiss, Terence Holt, and Alison Kay were instrumental in molding my ideas about the threat of bankruptcy and its intersection with concerns in *Goblin Market*, the area of discussion here in Chapter 3.

In turn, Rossetti's work was influenced by various aspects of her life including her family, her extensive reading, her religious faith, and her association with the artistic community in 19th-century England. These influences significantly shape her text and therefore need to be delineated to comprehend the full extent of Rossetti's contribution to literature:

1. Christina Rossetti's Homelife

Christina Rossetti's life was devoted to her parents. She never married; she became the caretaker and companion to her ailing parents, particularly her father whom she nursed for many years, as Jan Marsh indicates in *Christina Rossetti: A Writer's Life* (30). Rossetti was very close to her mother throughout their lives. Christina Rossetti's mother, Frances, attracted to the rituals and choral music of the Oxford Movement, began to attend Christ Church on Albany Street in 1843, accompanied by Christina and Maria, Christina's older sister (55). Christina Rossetti attended Christ Church for twenty years and during this time published *Maude, Goblin Market and Other Poems*, and *The Prince's Progress and Other Poems*, as Mary Arseneau reveals (*Symbol and Sacrament* 27). This is significant since Gabriele Rossetti, Christina Rossetti's father, was a devout Catholic, as David LoTempio explains (75). However, Gabriele Rossetti allowed the religious training of his children to be conducted by his wife.

Since her father was at times an evasive presence in her life except as an invalid needing Christina Rossetti's care, Rossetti turned to her Eternal Father for guidance. It is therefore not surprising that Christ as father, lover, and savior and Eve as the ultimate mother figure would figure prominently in her poetry. Therefore, Christina Rossetti's view of male/female relationships became disengaged from her understanding of her father and brothers (the influence of her brother Dante Gabriel Rossetti, which was considerable, on Christina Rossetti's works will be discussed in the section on the PreRaphaelite Brotherhood) as caretakers of women or of herself as their caretaker and instead became focused on the connection between Christ and women as caretakers of human spiritual health.

According to Georgina Battiscombe, Christina Rossetti did have a number of suitors and she did become engaged in 1848 to James Collinson, a lesser member of the Pre-Raphaelite Brotherhood and a member of the Catholic Church (47). He decided to become an Anglican because of his involvement with Christina Rossetti. Rossetti did not love him and when he renounced the Anglican Church and decided to rejoin the Catholic Church in Rome in 1850, their engagement was broken. A second proposal of marriage came in 1866 from Charles Bagot Cayley, a former student of Christina Rossetti's father (121). She denied his proposal because of his agnosticism (127). Similarly, in Rossetti's poem "The Iniquity of the Fathers Upon the Children" (1865), an illegitimate child "decides never to marry so that no man will have the power to assign her an identity," as Kristine Ann O'Reardon observes (30). Also, Laura loses her ability to define herself in *Goblin Market* when she gives in to the temptation of the goblin men and sells her soul for the "forbidden fruit" (O'Reardon 31).

The innocent woman in Rossetti's poetry represents the ideal Victorian woman, meek and submissive, especially to the men in the woman's life. In contrast, Rossetti speaks metaphorically of the fallen woman in many of her poems including *Goblin Market*, "What Would I Give," "Life and Death," "Cousin Kate," and "The Convent Threshold." Rossetti felt that marriage brought her farther away from her relationship with Christ. Marriage represented "fallen" status, falling away from the path to Grace (through participating in Christ's sufferings), and instead, giving in to the temptations of the flesh and of worldly vanities. Jerome McGann discusses the illusion of worldly love and marriage in Rossetti's works which encourage women to become dependent on men instead of on Christ (240).

This dependency on men is associated to deceptions, fears, and exploitation in Rossetti's writings. This fallacy was part of the corruption of the material world that women should be suspicious of and which is exemplified in many of Rossetti's poems including *Goblin Market*. Rossetti's poetry reflects her belief that it was the goal of every woman to "address the personal state of her soul" (Lo Tempio 157). The Victorian woman could not relate as a Christian to others without first looking to her own sins and finding the love of Christ in her own life. The soul's absolution for every woman is the final concern in most of her poetry (158). By embracing the "creator" inside herself, either through the imagination and or through motherhood, a woman finds this peace.

Although Christina Rossetti did not personally embrace motherhood as a life choice, she saw the significance of motherhood for the female descendants of Eve. Motherhood, as depicted in the character of Sin in Milton's *Paradise Lost* is poisonous. Motherhood is not toxic, as Janet Adelman argues (30), but nurturing in Christina Rossetti's poetry. This is evident at the end of *Goblin Market*. Christina Rossetti admired the literary contributions of Elizabeth Barrett Browning. Rossetti's view of motherhood in relation to the fallen woman is similar to Elizabeth Barrett Browning's depiction of the fallen woman and illegitimate mother Marian Erle, in the verse-novel *Aurora Leigh*. Marian Erle "is drugged, raped, and impregnated, but nevertheless remains essentially pure and a loving mother of her illegitimate child" (Browning xxii). Aurora Leigh, the central character, is on a quest in the book to find her place as a "creator" (woman and artist).

Aurora Leigh's meetings with Marian Erle's character as a fallen woman assist Aurora Leigh with this quest to retain purity in the face of corruption. Christina Rossetti's works revolve around this same idea of purifying sin and resisting temptation. The fallen woman figures prominently in Rossettis works also; the figure of Mary Magdalene, another fallen woman like Eve, appears in *The Face of the Deep*, "Mary Magdalene," "Mary Magdalene and the Other Mary," and *Time Flies*. In fact, "Magdalene" was a synonym for a reformed prostitute in Victorian England, as Diane D'Amico indicates ("Eve, Mary, and Mary Magdalene

. . ." 186). Christina Rossetti's works replicate the themes of the innocent struggling to remain pure and the fallen wishing to be redeemed.

2. Dante Alighieri's Influence

In William Rossetti's memoir of his older sister, Christina Rossetti, he reveals that his sister loved the writings of Plato, Shelley, Coleridge, Tennyson, and Elizabeth Barrett Browning, but she loved Dante's writing above all others (lxx). In Marsh's *A Writer's Life*, the author indicates that Christina Rossetti was an admirer of Dante's *The Divine Comedy*, as was her father, her brother Dante, and her sister Maria (Marsh 21). Swinburne once remarked that Dante worshippers "allowed no other gods on Parnassus . . . for these [people] there is but one Muse, and Dante is [their] prophet . . . [they may not] offer sacrifice to any other great Christian . . . poet such as Milton," as Edmund Gosse and Thomas Wise explain (109). Christina Rossetti privileged Dante's works over Milton's. In fact, as Jerome Bump asserts, Christina Rossetti's poem "The Convent Threshold" is deliberately modeled after Dante's *Divine Comedy* (338). Also, Christina Rossetti's sonnet sequence *Monna Innominata* uses quotations from Dante and Petrarch to begin each sonnet in the series.

Dante's *Divine Comedy* is written like a personal narrative, full of intense feelings, Herbert Smith discusses (27). Christina Rossetti's own personal way of expressing her religious fervor ran parallel to this description of Dante's work. His work has a sense of light and dark, reflected also in the Pre-Raphaelite preoccupation with this quality in their paintings. Christina Rossetti often pictured the world of vanity in her poetry and prose with the same sense of despair as in Dante's writing. For Christina Rossetti, Milton's classical allusions, especially in reference to Eve, ran in opposition to the medieval iconography of Dante's work. The medieval iconography in Dante's works most notably influences Rossetti's *Goblin Market*. The symbolism in this work takes on a Tractarian, sacramental quality. Christina Rossetti's work definitely displays imagination in poetry as a blend of Dantesque, Pre-Raphaelite, and Tractarian aesthetics (LoTempio 74).

3. Tractarian Influence

In her poetry and prose, Christina Rossetti imitated the ornamental and sacramental form that is characteristic of the writings of the leading Tractarians: John Henry Newman, John Keble, John Ruskin, and Isaac Williams, as LoTempio delineates

(2). The imagery practiced by the Pre-Raphaelite Brotherhood closely parallels the aesthetics in the writing of the Oxford Movement. In July of 1833, the Oxford Movement was officially born when Keble gave a sermon that stated that liberalism attacked the foundations of the High Church of England (4). The people who supported Keble and Newman's theological stance were called Tractarians; they upheld the beliefs of the Church of England. Christ was their personal savior.

The only true sacraments were Baptism and the Eucharist according to Tractarian faith (LoTempio 10). Baptism washed away the stain of the original sin brought about by Eve's fall from grace. The sacrament of the Eucharist, symbolically consuming the body and drinking the blood of Christ the savior of mankind, filled the void of desire created by Eve's sin. Participating in the Eucharist also represented the bond of sisterhood and brotherhood for all Tractarian believers. Every person was viewed as a sinner who was shadowed by Eve's disobedience but who could be redeemed as Eve was through repentance. "Everything necessary for salvation could be found in scripture" (11). The focus of the Oxford Movement was that it was a Christian writer's revolution (70). A fellow student of Keble's, John Henry Newman, became the soul of this religious movement. A series of Newman's sermons and essays were published in pamphlets and entitled *The Tracts of the Times*; therefore, the followers of this religious movement became known as Tractarians (71). Communion with God was emphasized in the Tracts.

Christina Rossetti was born in 1830 just as the philosophy and preaching of Newman, Keble and Froude was becoming popular at Oxford, as Katherine J. Mayberry discusses (4). Although her writings postdate the fervor of the Oxford Movement, the inspiration of these Anglicans lived on in the writings of people like Christina Rossetti (LoTempio 74). In fact, G. B. Tennyson stated in *Victorian Devotional Poetry: The Tractarian Mode* that "Christina Rossetti is the true inheritor of the Tractarian devotional mode in poetry. Most of what the Tractarians advocated in theory and sought to put into practice came to fruition in the poetry of Christina Rossetti" (198).

Christina Rossetti's devotional poetry deals with the relationship between Eve, Christ, and the daughters of Eve and is similar to the religious poetry of the Tractarians, like John Keble's *The Christian Year*. She read this book often and kept it at her bedside (LoTempio 81). According to Linda Schofield, *The Christian Year* concentrates on human isolation from God and leads the reader "through a personal quest toward union with God and cognizance of His Word" (302). Rossetti's poetry reflects the Tractarian belief that we all move from "isolation in the temporal world and ignorance of its meaning to a recognition that the divine reality not only includes [us] but makes sense of it all" (303). Rossetti saw Eve as the first woman dealing with this sense of alienation and exploring her relationship with God. Tractarian poetry often uses the rhetorical strategy of question and answer to explore this union with God's Word. Rossetti's poems "Bird or Beast?" "What Would I Give?" and "Who Shall Deliver Me?" follow this format. Alienation from God is also contemplated in Christina Rossetti's poem "A Better Resurrection" which ends with the line "O Jesus, drink of me" (l. 24), as R. W. Crump reveals (68). The speaker in the poem discovers eternal life, given to mankind by Christ's sacrifice and celebrated in the Eucharist. The speaker in the poem identifies with the chalice and the wine and in this way, becomes one with the Deity. These lines are reminiscent of her poem *Goblin Market* where the Tractarian belief in the sacrament of the Eucharist is tied to Christina Rossetti's interest in sisterhood as part of the creation/redemption cycle. The love relationship, the mystical union between God and the redeemed, sets the postulant free.

The members of the Oxford Movement believed in God's munificence, as LoTempio indicates (42). An appreciation of but also a skepticism towards the details of the natural world is a precept of Pre-Raphaelite and Tractarian belief systems. This absorption with the vanity of the natural world is directly related to the fall of Eve in Eden. In poems like "An Apple Gathering," "Another Spring," "The First Spring Day," "A Better Resurrection," "Sweet Death," "Dream-Love," and "L.E.L." Christina Rossetti displays this absorption with God's natural abundance and also the irony of living wholly obsessed in that world of vanity.

Milton's Eve falls, in part, due to her abuse of imagination. The Tractarians, however, saw imagination concentrated on the symbols of Christ as assistance for the soul to rise to Heaven. Imagination did not "lead humanity away from the Lord through deceitful illusions of the mind" (LoTempio 51) as long as piety directed the imagination towards heaven and not towards the material world as it did with Eve. The conflict in Christina Rossetti's poetry often hinges on these two views of imagination, the sensual versus the divine, reworking Milton's vision of temptation in the form of imagination. Rossetti believed, as is evident in her poetry, that Eve was predestined to succumb to imagination's temptation so that she could perform her function in the universal creation chain with Christ.

In this way, the Oxford Movement was associated with the concept of imagination in writing (LoTempio 70). The Tractarians believed that "the creation of poetry was a religious activity analogous to the work of God," the ultimate "creator," as Mayberry asserts (128). Another aspect to God's work that the members of the Tractarian community adhered to was an obligation to guide others to the proper path. Tractarianism fostered sisterhood and brotherhood. It is not surprising that much of Christina Rossetti's life, which is reflected in her poetry, was centered on volunteer work such as her charity work in the home for fallen women, her work with factory girls, her protests against vivisection, and her devotion to ailing family members (LoTempio 77). Her religious poetry and her social, community volunteer work were examples of her Christian faith in action; she believed that it was the mission of the daughters of Eve to unite all women.

The High Anglican church supported "the establishment of sisterhoods allowing women to escape from the restrictive work of the home in order to take on significant [spiritual] responsibility," as Antony H. Harrison professes ("Christina Rossetti and the Sage Discourse . . ." 100). Christina Rossetti was attracted to the life of sisterhood, and her older sister, Maria, entered the community of All Saints Sisterhood on Margaret Street in 1874; this community was founded in 1851, as Thomas Jay Williams and Allan Walter Campbell observe (26). The concept of sisterhood tied all women to each other as the daughters of Eve.

Rossetti's view of sisterhood is connected to her vision of Eve's role and the roles of the daughters of Eve in the creation cycle. Christina Rossetti's use of Tractarian tenets affected the development of her vision of Eve from her early poetry (1846 to 1860) to *Goblin Market* written in 1859 to her poetry and prose concerning Eve and the daughters of Eve written from 1860 to 1894. "The Convent Threshold" and "Three Nuns" like *Goblin Market* reveal that there is greater fidelity in Christ than through earthly love, that the impure soul, like Eve's, can be cleansed of decay by Christ's love (LoTempio 130). By experiencing the benefits of the "sisterhood" in each of these poems, a woman can become closer to Christ and therefore closer to the first mother, Eve. Love is fully consummated, however, in the "sacramental domain" of heaven, as LoTempio expostulates (131). Love in the earthly world is transient. This world of sisterhood is another quality Christina Rossetti found lacking in Milton's *Paradise Lost*.

4. Pre-Raphaelite Influence

Christina Rossetti was also greatly influenced by the brotherhood called the Pre-Raphaelites. Because it was named the Pre-Raphaelite Brotherhood, all women were naturally excluded from membership despite the fact that Christina Rossetti was a major contributing figure to their literary publication *The Germ* and often was the subject who sat for the portraits they painted (along with her mother), including Dante Gabriel's *The Girlhood of Mary Virgin*, as Bump explains (324). "The first literary victory for the Pre-Raphaelites was the publication of *'Goblin Market' and Other Poems*, and it was written by the member [of the group] they excluded" (324).

The Pre-Raphaelites "combined a reverence for ritual and tradition with an interest in creating images from biblical history that revised many of the current assumptions of aesthetic practice," as Cynthia Scheinberg indicates (9). These works of art shared a Ruskinian kind of richness of ornamentation and a vivid use of color with a strange, illuminative sense of light that is also apparent in Christina Rossetti's poetry. Ruskin believed that "the artist must be careful in presenting the detail of nature in order to convey its transcendental truth" (Harrison, Anthony, *Christina Rossetti in Context* 29). The diaphanous quality of objects and light in Pre-Raphaelite art and in Christina Rossetti's poetry, representing the presence of God reflected in worldly materialism and nature, is derived from this concept. According to LoTempio, this relates to John Keble's idea that nature was a hieroglyph of the divine world (LoTempio 82). Ruskin described Typical Beauty, related to the material world, and Vital Beauty, related to the abstract world of moral truths, as important aspects to Pre-Raphaelite painting.

Christina Rossetti's poetry duplicates Ruskin's vision of beauty in the world. The Pre-Raphaelites manifesto included the love of nature's plentitude, a rebellion against simplistic dualisms or symbolism, worship of medievalism or Romanticism, and a preference for morbid subject matter or melancholy as the source of creativity. All of these are mirrored in Christina Rossetti's Eve poetry. There was a unity and oneness of all things in Rossetti's poetry, tied not only to God but to the mother of mankind, Eve. Nature is depicted in Rossetti's poetry as part of the cycle of the female existence. The dream of heaven's garden, paralleled with the garden of Eden, is often the theme in Christina Rossetti's poems and reflects the influence of the writing of Dante Alighieri on her work.

Scheinberg asserts that the vast amount of literary criticism on Christina Rossetti often fails to define Rossetti's poetic identity as an amalgamation of religion, gender and aesthetics (243). Critics adeptly define her in terms of one construct but not successfully in all three. This author would agree. However, it is not Rossetti's link of the Hebraic and Christian female poet that characterizes Christina Rossetti, as Scheinberg would have you believe, but Rossetti's devotion, as Eve's daughter, to each Victorian woman's role in the Christian creation cycle which combines Rossetti's perspectives on religion, gender, and aesthetics so cohesively.

In the first chapter of this book, I will discuss how Christina Rossetti's fixation with eyes and sight is a manifestation not just of her religious beliefs and aesthetic principles but more importantly her lifelong fascination with Plato's discussion of "the Eye of the Mind" in *The Republic*.

CHAPTER 1

"The Eye of the Mind" in Christina Rossetti's Poetry

Christina Rossetti's life and written works were characterized by a preoccupation with eyes. In her youth, Christina Rossetti's eyes were bright and alert, an azure-grey that sometimes deepened into a velvety grey, as Elizabeth Luther Cary indicates (241). Rossetti's personality was revealed in her eyes (244). However, in 1871, Rossetti was stricken with a disease that changed her appearance. She lived for 23 more years and during that time she retained the symptom of this disease: a protrusion of the eyeballs (240). During these years, she usually veiled her eyes from strangers.

Christina Rossetti's sister Maria could be phobic when it came to looking and seeing. Just before Maria entered the convent, Rossetti and her sister had visited the British Museum. Maria Rossetti refrained from becoming part of the sight-seers who looked at the mummies "because she realized how the general resurrection might happen" (231). Maria also would not look on some prints from the Book of Job which "went counter to the Second Commandment" (Cary 232).

Christina Rossetti was not the only female writer from the English Victorian age who was interested in the concept of sight. In Joyce Zonana's essay "The Embodied Muse," she discusses Elizabeth Barrett Browning's poetic book *Aurora Leigh*. The character Aurora Leigh is woman and artist, poet and muse in the book, and her beloved Romney can only see the subjectified Aurora Leigh after he becomes blind. He represents the idea of the blind poet, embodied in Homer and Milton (252).

One year before Christina Rossetti wrote *Goblin Market*, she and her mother sat for a portrait by her brother Dante Gabriel entitled *The Girlhood of Mary Virgin*, as Garlick observes (113). Christina Rossetti posed for the figure of the Virgin Mary in the painting, with eyes downcast in humility and subjugation. "The Virgin was not just a receptacle for God's seed but was an active participant in the creative process" (113). This portrait is the quintessence of Pre-Raphaelite creation, exhibiting the innocence and spiritual transcendence of the Virgin Mary and at the same time, revealing the erotic sensuality of the material world juxtaposed to the moral world of the righteous. Christina Rossetti's poetry debates these same issues through similar imagery. The appetites of the reader are tempted, and focus on the strength of morality in sisterhood and devotion to Christ's earthly example is emphasized as a way to combat life's temptations.

According to Jan Marsh in *Pre-Raphaelite Women: Images of Femininity*, in 1848, the same year that Rossetti posed for her brother's painting, Christina Rossetti also posed for James Collinson's personal portrait of her (42). Christina Rossetti is delineated as diminutive and meek with eyes averted (42). These paintings represent the existence of the seer and the seen, the eye and what the eye symbolizes and perceives. The "eye" as the organ of the perception of reality cannot "conceive" what the individual's imagination can create. The "conception" of the "eye" also directly relates to the idea of the separated self, the creator and procreator represented in the Pre-Raphaelite paintings Rossetti sat for. "This is the dichotomy, the portrait of two female characters, as it appears in *Goblin Market*," as Vickie Jan Smith explains (35). Laura is the artist and Lizzie is the procreator. The poem concludes with the procreator, Lizzie, saving the artist Laura from her risk-taking adventures with the goblin men.

In another painting by Dante Rossetti, "Hesterna Rosa," Christina is posed in a bacchanalian setting, similar to the plot of *Goblin Market*; she is looking away from frame with her eyes covered by her outstretched hand (Garlick 114). Garlick asserts that "Rossetti's presence is carefully controlled. . .[the] figure is inhibited in her sensuality, covering her face
. . . with a flowery coronet serving to bind her hair rather than loosely sitting on freed hair like the other, more abandoned female figure [in the portrait]" (114). A scene of seduction is depicted. There are two men in the portrait. The woman with the loose hair is enjoying the company of one of the men; she is sitting in his lap and a monkey is nearby. The woman in the portrait that Rossetti sat for is resisting the temptation of food, drink, and lascivious play that the other man in the painting is enticing her with by looking away with her hand over her eyes, blocking out the sensuality of reality.

Christina Rossetti's poetry and prose reflect this predilection towards the subject of eyes and sight. There have been a number of scholarly publications on the subject, interrogating Rossetti's "eye" fixation in her writings, over the past two decades. For example, in Dolores Rosenblum's article "Christina Rossetti's Religious Poetry," Rosenblum, examining theories also discussed in Michel Foucault's *The Order of Things*, asserts that visual metaphor is central to Rossetti's conception of self in her poetry and prose; seeing stands for knowing, loving, and having.

Religious scripture has many examples of who is seen and who sees. Adam and Eve in Genesis are an example of the man who gazes upon his beloved's face that is supposed to mirror his soul. This is also a Petrarchan convention, woman as the object of the gaze, the focus of poetic vision. A female poet like Christina Rossetti would speak from a fragmented poetic consciousness; the female poet is an observer and also the observed in a patriarchal culture. The female poet embodies both of these roles when she writes. Christina Rossetti often posed for her brother, Dante Gabriel, when he painted. His female models look blind, transfixed or sphinx-like in his paintings; this way of viewing women objectifies them.

Catherine Maxwell asserts in "Tasting the 'Fruit Forbidden': Gender, Intertextuality, and Christina Rossetti's *Goblin Market*" that Rossetti's obsession with the eye has to do with her Tractarian faith, that seeing equals temptation. The eyes consume things that harm the soul. The fall from innocence comes from looking. Maxwell applies this idea to texts. Reading texts is an "in-corporation." Diane D'Amico agrees with Catherine Maxwell and observes in D'Amico's book *Christina Rossetti: Faith, Gender, and Time* that *Goblin Market* is not about facing the goblin men as Lizzie does; it is about not looking at the goblin men which is what Laura does, because seeing is consumption. D'Amico uses Alfred, Lord Tennyson's "The Lady of Shalott" as another example of this idea. The lady looks at the real world through a mirror. She does not look at reality. Rossetti believed that religion was the way to see the material world clearly.

Esther T. Hu discusses in her research John Keble's focus on the "divine gaze" in his tracts and Christina Rossetti's interpretation of the "divine gaze" in her poetry and prose. Christine Wiesenthal is concerned with how Rossetti's poem "Reflection" relates to Jacques Lacan's concept of the "gaze" from a 20th-century perspective and how Lacan's ideas show historical significance as a researcher looks back at Rossetti's poetry. Reading Rossetti through the writings of Lacan is Suzy Waldman's project as well, analyzing Rossetti's stolen images and visions in her writing.

Lorraine Janzen Kooistra argues that Rossetti's obsession with eyes is related to a concern with death, that the dead have eyes that are shut by a mortician. When someone dies, their eyes are open but unseeing, as Kooistra ponders (*Christina Rossetti and Illustration* 34). Kooistra relates this idea to Laura and Lizzie in *Goblin Market* as a response to Angela Leighton's reading of Rossetti's works in relation to closed eyes as a figurative death for women in Victorian society who had no control over identity or power. Kooistra also writes about the significance of the envisionment of Rossetti's *Goblin Market* by illustrators throughout the decades (143, 145, 147, 149, 151, 153, 155, 156, 160, 164) including Rossetti's brother, Dante Gabriel (1862), Dion Clayton Calthrop (1906), Margaret W. Tarrant (1912), Arthur Rackham (1933), Kinuko Craft (1973), Laurence Housman (1893), George Gershinowitz (1981), Marin Ware (1980), John Bolton (1984), and Florence Harrison (1910).

Mary Wilson Carpenter interrogates a queer studies interpretation of *Goblin Market* in her essay "'Eat Me, Drink Me, Love Me': The Consumable Female Body in Christina Rossetti's *Goblin Market*" in which she discusses Rossetti's use of what is seen and not seen in the poem. Carpenter believes that the representation of the sisterhood of the female gaze feasting upon the female form is a desire for the maternal body. McGann indicates in "Christina Rossetti's Poems: a New Edition and Re-evaluation" that Rossetti wrestled with the central moral problem in a symbolically ordered world: distinguishing what seems from what is (237). Although I agree with McGann that Rossetti is concerned with the difference between illusion and reality, I believe the central foundation to these allusions in her writings have to do with her fascination with Plato.

What all of these discussions, concerning Rossetti's literary observations on the eye, lack is a concentrated examination of Rossetti's interest in Plato and Plato's "Eye of the Mind." Christina Rossetti has well aware of Plato's writings. During her time as an adult spent at Brookbank in Surrey (she was there to visit relatives and friends and meet with admirers of her writings), Rossetti read a volume of Plato offered by her hostess to stimulate thought (Marsh *A Writer's Life* 313). While Rossetti was ill, she wintered at Hastings and read the six-volume Bohn edition of Plato she had received as a birthday gift (319).

In middle age, she formulated a mystical vision of life after death from her readings of Plato; her ideas on Christian Platonism absorbed much of her time and her writing (342). "Rossetti read and re-read Plato with absorption" (357), often lending out her copy of what she called "the glorious *Apology, Crito* and *Phaedo*" to her friends. Rossetti's brother, William Michael Rossetti, states in his memoir of his sister that "among very great authors, none (making allowance for Dante) seemed to appeal to her more than Plato: she read his *Dialogues* over and over again, with ever renewed or augmented zeal" (lxx). So, it is clear that Rossetti had done close readings of Plato's works (Marsh *A Writer's Life* 458), including "The Allegory of the Cave" from *The Republic* in which Plato discusses the concept of "the Eye of the Mind."

Plato's The Allegory of the Cave"

"The Allegory of the Cave" is a fictional dialogue between Plato's teacher Socrates and Plato's brother Glaucon, at the beginning of Book 7 of Plato's *Republic*. Socrates begins by describing a scenario in which what people take to be real would in fact be an illusion. He asks Glaucon to imagine a cave inhabited by prisoners who have been chained and held immobile since childhood: not only are their arms and legs held in place, but their heads are also fixed, compelled to gaze at a wall in front of them. Behind the prisoners is an enormous fire, and between the fire and the prisoners is a raised walkway, along which people walk carrying things on their heads "including figures of animals made of wood and stone and various materials" (qtd in Damrosch 713).

The prisoners watch the shadows cast by the men, not knowing they are shadows. There are also echoes off the wall from the noise produced from the walkway. Socrates suggests the prisoners would take the shadows to be real things and the echoes to be real sounds, not just reflections of reality, since they are all they had ever seen or heard. They would praise as clever whoever could best guess which shadow would come next, as someone who understood the nature of the world, and the whole of their society would depend on the shadows on the wall. Socrates next introduces something new to this scenario: suppose that a prisoner is freed and permitted to stand up. If someone were to show him the things that had cast the shadows, he would not recognize them for what they were and could not name them; he would believe the shadows on the wall to be more real than what he sees.

Then Socrates says, "and if he is compelled to look straight at the light, will he not have a pain in his eyes which will make him turn away to take refuge in the objects of vision which he can see, and which he will conceive to be in reality clearer than the things which are now being showm to him?" (713). What if someone forcibly dragged such a man upward, out of the cave: wouldn't the man be angry at the one doing this to him? And if dragged all the way out into the sunlight, wouldn't he be distressed and unable to see "even one of the things now said to be true" like the shadows on the wall? (qtd in Damrosch 713). After some time on the surface, however, Socrates suggests that the freed prisoner would acclimate. He would see more and more things around him, until he could look upon the Sun. He would understand that the Sun is the source of the seasons and the years, and is the steward of all things in the visible place, and is in a certain way the cause of all those things he and his companions had been seeing (714).

Socrates next asks Glaucon to consider the condition of this man. "And when he remembered his old habitation, and the wisdom of the den andd his fellow-prisoners, do you not suppose that he woruld felictate himself on the change, and pity them" (714). Glaucon concurs. Socrates continues, "And if they were in the habit of conferring honours among themselves on those who were quickest to observe the passing shadows and to remark which of them went before and which followed after, and which were together; and who were therefore best able to draw conclusions as to the future, do you think that he would care for such hours and glories, or envy the possessers of them? And Glaucon remarks that he would feel pity for his fellow-prisoners and the ignorance of their state (qtd in Damrosch 714). Socrates goes on to relate that if were he to return to the cave or den, he would be rather bad at their game, no longer being accustomed to the darkness. His fellows would say that he went up and came back with his eyes corrupted, and that it's not even worth trying to go up because of his malady (714). If they were somehow able to get their hands on and kill the man who attempts to release and lead up, they would try to kill him.

Plato, in *The Republic*, uses the sun as a metaphor for the source of "illumination," arguably intellectual illumination, which he held to be the form or idea of the Good which is sometimes interpreted as Plato's notion of God, the "universal author" and "lord of light" (714-5). The metaphor is about the nature of ultimate reality and how we come to know it. Socrates is the speaker of *The Republic*, but it is generally believed that the thoughts expressed are Plato's:

> The prison-house is the world of sight, the light of the fire is the sun, and you will not misapprehend me if you interpret the journey upwards to be the ascent of the soul into the intellectual world [. . .] in the world of knowledge the idea of good appears last of all, and is seen only with an effort; and when seen, is also inferred to be the universal author of all things beautiful and right, parent of light and of the lord of light in the

visible world, and the immediate source of reason and truth in the intellectual. (qtd in Damrosche 714)

The eye, Plato says, is unusual among the sense organs in that it needs a medium, namely light, in order to operate. The are two causes of seeing: "from coming out of the light or from going into the light, which is true of the mind's eye, quite as much as of the bodily eye" (715). The strongest and best source of light is the sun; with it, we can discern objects clearly. Plato also says the sun and the Good ("the object of knowledge") are both sources of "generation":

> The sun [. . .] not only furnishes to those that see the power of visibility but it also provides for their generation and growth and nurture though it is not itself generation. [. . .] In like manner, then [. . .] the objects of knowledge not only receive from the presence of the good their being known, but their very existence and essence is derived to them from it, though the good itself is not essence but still transcends essence in dignity and surpassing power. (qtd in Damrosch 715)

This is one of the passages that leads some to infer that the Good is, for Plato, God. Plato calls the Good, the source of being (the being of the forms, at least), something that (somehow) sheds light on all other forms, and a universal.

"Plato's third eye," according to an ancient anecdote, was an eye Plato dreamt he had grown after he had discovered the theory of ideas. In Marsilio Ficino's reinterpretation of it, as James Hankins discusses, it was an eye located in the center of Plato's forehead by which he perceived divine things - the eye of the mind, in other words. Plato believed in dualism, that the mind and body were separate. Imagination is often called "the mind's eye" and the Tractarians, like Rossetti, connected imagination to God; it was a gift from God that was to be used to reflect the glory of Christ and his teachings.

In Plato's "The Allegory of the Cave," he suggests that there are two different forms of vision, a "mind's eye" and a "bodily eye" (Damrosch 715). The "bodily eye" is a metaphor for the senses. While inside the cave, the prisoners function only with this eye. The "mind's eye" is a higher level of thinking, and is mobilized only when the prisoner is released into the outside world. This eye does not exist within the cave; it only exists in the real, perfect world. The "bodily eye" relies on sensory perceptions about the world in order to determine what is reality. Metaphorically speaking, the cave is a physical world filled with imperfect images. This world is filled with distorted images about reality. Inside the cave, the prisoners believe that the shadows they see on the wall are actual reality. Their "bodily eye" tells them that this world is real because their senses perceive so. Plato suggests that the senses do not perceive actual truth.

The "mind's eye" is not active inside the cave because the prisoners are imprisoned in this distorted world, which they believe is reality. When one prisoner is pulled out of the cave and into the light of the sun, it is this sudden freedom that starts the gradual process of enlightenment. This sudden freedom opens the "mind's eye."

Rossetti uses the word "sun" as a play on words for the "son," the son of God, Jesus Christ in her poetry; Christ is the focus of her religious poetry because Jesus Christ was the center of Tractarian faith and beliefs. Christ is the source of light and knowledge. An example of how Rossetti uses light and fire as metaphors to discuss Plato's allegory appears in Rossetti's prose work *The Face of the Deep*:

> So sparks fly upward scaling heaven by fire,
>
> Still mount and still attain not, yet draw nigher
>
> While they have being to their fountain flame.
>
> To saints who mount, the bottomless abyss
>
> Is as mere nothing; they have set their face
>
> Onward and upward toward that blessed place
>
> Where man rejoices with his God . . . (460)

Constance Hassett indicates that Christina Rossetti "takes Biblical fire as 'a figure' for meditation" (223). The earthly fire of the cave that Plato discusses does not hinder a true believer of in-sight; in-sight aids a believer in focusing on the real object of the gaze, the light of the son -- Christ's love and forgiveness for the dead and/or martyred. One of the prayers in *Face of the Deep* asks the holy spirit to "purge our eyes to discern and contemplate thee; until we attain to see as thou seest, judge as thou judgest, choose as thou choosest, and having sought and found thee, to behold thee forever and forever" (13). There is a private and a public gaze. The eyes purged of the public gaze, the shadows of so-called reality, can then truly see the truth, the enlightenment of Christ's teachings.

In another passage of *Face of the Deep*, Rossetti compares Plato's "shadows" to in-sight:

> Shadows to-day, while shadows show God's Will.
>
> Light were not good except He sent us light.
>
> Shadows today, because this day is night. (166)

Andrew Armond discusses Rossetti's usage of shadow and light in *Face of the Deep*. "There is an inherent paradox in the image of a shadow "show[ing]" anything, since shadows are inherently concealing. But Rossetti utilizes this paradoxical image to demonsterate that God's will is revealed by shadows" (Armond 238). Only by knowing the shadows inside the cave can the released prisoner in Plato's allegory understand the difference between shadows made by the fire in the cave and the light burning from the sun. Only by knowing the shadows of the world can one discover the true meaning of the object of the gaze, the light that comes from focusing on the "eye of the mind."

Rossetti's fascination with eyes is also connected to the Victorian fixation on Orientalism. Although art and design in Victorian England was influenced by many sources including most famously English Medieval art and culture, there was another strong influence that affected Victorian thinking and lifestyle in England. "Victorientalism" is a contemporary term used to describe the fixation English Victorian culture had on Eastern countries and cultures. The Imperialist regime of Queen Victoria's reign imposed English rule over countries like India for decades. Imperialism was about restructuring native culture by "Westernizing" it, making Eastern cultures more like Western European culture. This was a racist agenda since there were those in Victorian England who felt Occidental culture was the best and preferred culture. Nonetheless, English Victorian scholars like Alfred, Lord Tennyson and Benajmin Jowett were fascinated with Eastern culture (Livingston 163).

This fixation on all things Eastern permeated Victorian society from architecture to jewelry. *Japonisme* or *Japonaiserie* are terms used to describe the assimilation of art and design in Victorian England of Japanese aesthetics, as Ayako Ono asserts (2). Dante Gabriel Rossetti, Rossetti's older brother, was a "Japoniste"; he was a collector, distributor, and supporter of Japanese art and design. "These cultural interests and assimilations, which also included Chinese, Moorish, Persian, Indian, and Javanese styles, instigated a blurring of cultural lines under the umbrella term "Oriental," and received attention in various International Exhibitions in most notably 1862, 1871, 1873 and 1878" in Victorian England (Ono 28). Arthur Liberty opened East India House in London in 1875 (11); Morris, Ruskin, Burne-Jones, Rossetti all collected Eastern art and artifacts by being customers of Liberty's shop (68). In a recent BBC broadcast, Navid Akhar indicated that William Morris and other artists from the Pre-Raphaelite brotherhood were influenced by Islamic art and its design elements.

It is therefore likely that Christina Rossetti, with her ties to the cutting edge artists of the Pre-Raphaelite brotherhood, would be aware of Eastern mythology and philosophy since this was a major trend among artists and philosophers during the time period when Rossetti was alive. There are a number of Eastern philosophies and beliefs that are associated with the "eye of the mind" or the "third eye." Many of these traditions have to do with eyes being closed. Rossetti's writing is saturated with images of the Christian faithful whose eyes are closed. The closed eyes not only represent a refusal to look on temptation and the vanity of the world but more importantly, closed eyes assist the person in focusing on the "eye of the mind."

Hindus place a mark or colored dot on the forehead referred to as "tilaka," "bottu," bindiya," kumkum," or "bindi." This dot is a sign of piety revealing that the wearer is a Hindu. It symbolizes the third eye – the eye that is focused inwards on God. When the coin is put on a person's forehead after death, the coin covers up the "third eye" ("Hinduism" ReligiousTolerance.org 1). The god Shiva meditates with "the third eye" shut. The third eye is usually closed. The third eye looks inward. In the Hindu story of how the universe came into being, Shiva restored order to the world by forming a third eye in his forehead from which emerged fire to restore light. The light from the third eye is very powerful. If Shiva opens his third eye, anyone he looks upon (like the god Kama Ananga) is reduced to dust.

The colored marking that Hindus wear depicting the third eye represents Shiva's third eye. In the Hindu faith, creation follows destruction. Shiva is considered the representative of power that restores what has been dissolved ("Hinduism" Reference.com 1). So, in Eastern and Western interpretations of the third eye, the "eye of the mind" is the source of power and enlightenment, of growth, renewal and rebirth. When a person of the Hindu faith dies, the eyes of the body are closed and coins are placed on the forehead to buy a ticket to heaven or hell ("Indian Mirror – Culture – Rituals" 1). The tradition of putting a coin on the forehead probably originated with the ancient Greek tradition of covering the dead person's eyes with coins which were used to pay Charon to take the dead person across the river Styx to the land of the dead ("Amusing World: Rituals of the Dead" 1). The coin on the forehead would cover therefore the "third eye." Layman Seiken has said,

> There I was, hunched over office desk,
>
> Mind an unruffled pool.
>
> A thunderbolt! My middle eye
>
> Shot wide, revealing – my ordinary self. (Seiken 14)

Rossetti would agree with this, that when in a state of relaxation, the "eye of the mind" shows a person a reflection not of the public gaze, not of the outer world of vanity, but of the "ordinary self" in the face of God. Seiken's writing explains the essence of "eyes wide shut" from Rossetti's perspective. The bodily "eye" must be shut so that the "eye of the mind" can absorb in-sight.

The English Victorians, however, were not only interested in Hindu philosophy. The study of Buddhism became an obsession in late 19th-century England. Christina Rossetti was born in 1830 and died in 1894. These dates coincide precisely with the English interest in Buddhist principles, which started in the 1830s, "matured as a study of comparative religion in the 1860s, and peaked in the popular culture of London" in the 1890s, as Jeffrey Franklin observes (941). Numerous articles published in Victorian England offered accounts of the life of Buddha to a newly fascinated readership. Many of those contributed to what might be called the Victorian Jesus-versus-Buddha debate" (Franklin 943). Rossetti was a strict Tractarian; however, because of her close ties to the artistic community through her brother Dante Gabriel Rossetti, she would have been aware of this trend.

A number of poems were written about Buddhism during this time. Richard Phillips in his book-length poem *The Story of Gautama Buddha and his Creed: An Epic*, published in England in 1871, discusses "the luscious fruits that Eastern lands produce" (950). Sir Edwin Arnold's popular poem *The Light of Asia. Being the Life and Teaching of Gautama, Prince of India and Found of Buddhism*, published in 1879, created quite a societal stir and is noted for its catalog of exotic elements much like those included in Phillips' poem and much like the list of exotic fruits in Rossetti's *Goblin Market*.

Although Rossetti's masterpiece *Goblin Market* predates Phillips' and Arnold's poems, her poem features exotic enumerations and may be a response to the Eastern obsession in Western sensibility since her English heroine defeats the goblin men and their "wares." By shutting her eyes, Lizzie, a character in *Goblin Market*, can concentrate on the "eye of the mind" to obtain enlightenment. The imperialist agenda, the invasion and corruption of exotic lands by imposing Western values on Eastern cultures, is interrogated in *Goblin Market*. What Rossetti observes is that as England physically encroached on other nations, the other nations became a philosophical obsession with the English. Thus, the tables were turned and Orientalism philosophically "invaded" England. Rossetti's "eye" was not that of the Hindus nor of the Buddhists but a reaction to English Victorian obsession with Eastern cultures.

This obsession caused an intrusion of eastern culture into Western philosophy, disrupting Victorian "reality" by leading people towards speculation about Eastern religions and away from the true light of Christ which Rossetti believed was what Plato called "the Good." Rossetti believed as Plato discusses in his writings, through the voice of Socrates, that divine inspiration gives a person access to insights about reality. People who see with their eyes are blind; the senses do not give a person sight. The senses only show a den of evil and ignorance, as explained in *The Allegory of the Cave*. Those who travel the difficult path to enlightenment are ridiculed by those who do not travel the path. Ideas and imagination, targeted towards an understanding of Christ's teachings, are more powerful than the natural world.

Rossetti's poetry reflects Plato's theories about "the eye of the mind." Rossetti's poems and prose are saturated with the "I" and the "eye," with circles and cycles. Rossetti's "I" represents the "eye of the mind." The bodily "eye" perceives the material world of vanity which tempts the conscience; therefore, the bodily "eye" affects what the "I," "the eye of the mind" perceives to be real and good. Rossetti's "I" also reflects her Tractarian faith; the members of the Oxford Movement defined the "I" as the imagination that should devote manifestations of the imagination like artistic endeavors such as writing and painting to the glorification of Christ. In fact, the first person "I" appears in ninety percent of Christina Rossetti's poems. I believe this fixation on the word "I" is a manifestation of her perception of Plato's "eye of the mind."

The poems of Christina Rossetti written between 1847 and 1858 reveal her interest in Plato's theories. "Vanity of Vanities" (1847) is a perfect example. "Pleasure that bringeth sorrow at the last, / Glory that at the last bringeth no gain!" (ll. 3-4). The pleasures and glories of the world are all vanity. The word "vanity" to Rossetti represented the shadows on the cave wall in Plato's "The Allegory of the Cave." Pleasure and glory are sensual and experienced through the "bodily eye." The poem indicates that when Judgement day arrives all of peoples of the earth will realize that the pleasures and glories of the physical world are meaningless because only those things witnessed with "the eye of the mind" are truly important: "Yea, even the young shall answer sighingly / Saying one to another: How vain it is!" (Crump 1, 153, ll. 13-14):

> Ah, woe is me for pleasure that is vain,
> Ah, woe is me for glory that is pain:
> Pleasure that bringeth sorrow at the last,
> Glory that at the last bringeth no gain!
> So saith the sinking heart, and so again
> It shall say till the mighty angel-blast
> Is blown, making the sun and moon aghast
> And showering down the stars like sudden rain.
> And evermore men shall go fearfully
> Bending beneath their weight of heaviness;

> And ancient men shall lie down wearily,
> And strong men shall rise up in weariness;
> Yea, even the young shall answer sighingly
> Saying one to another: How vain it is! (Crump 1, 153)

The bodily "eye" and what it perceives to be the truth is a falsehood that only brings "woe," "weariness," and a "sinking heart" to the "seer." "The weight of heaviness" is the burden that mankind bears, relying only on the public gaze as the source of truth, just like the beings who are chained in the cave believe the shadows to be reality.

The uselessness of Plato's illusionary "shadows on the wall" are reiterated in Rossetti's sonnet "The One Certainty," published in June 1849 as William Rossetti explains (119):

> Vanity of vanities, the Preacher saith,
> All things are vanity. The eye and ear
> Cannot be filled with what they see and hear.
> Like early dew, or like the sudden breath
> Of wind, or like the grass that withereth
> Is man, tossed to and fro by hope and fear:
> So little joy hath he, so little cheer,
> Till all things end in the long dust of death.
> To-day is still the same as yesterday,
> To-morrow also even as one of them;
> And there is nothing new under the sun:
> Until the ancient race of Time be run,
> The old thorns shall grow out of the old stem,
> And morning shall be cold and twilight grey. (Crump 1, 72)

"The eye and ear / Cannot be filled with what they see and hear" (ll. 2-3): the senses do not give one enlightenment. The senses reveal a false sense of reality. What most people would call reality, the outer world of the senses, Rossetti believed was illusion just as the cave dwellers in Plato's "Allegory of the Cave" thought the shadows on the wall were reality. However, the person who escaped and saw the sun in the world above the cave realized that the world of enlightenment from the sun was the true reality. This is what Plato viewed as dualism, a separation of body and mind. Rossetti believed that in-sight, what the eye of the mind perceives, should be the object of the gaze and was the true reality, and the world of the senses was illusion. What fills one is not the outer world but the intellectual and spiritual illumination of in-sight. The senses only show us a "cold" and "grey" world of "thorns" and "dust." Only the light coming from the Good gives a person hope. The sensual world is one of despair and "fear."

There are actually two "certainties" in this poem. One is the certainty that all things "seen" by the senses are empty, and the other certainty that is implied is that all things "seen" through the enlightenment of The Good are lasting. In "Vanity of Vanities" and in "One Certainty," Rossetti refers to the sun. The sun is ever present; vanity is fleeting. The sun is always related to the "son" of God in Rossetti's works. Christ is omnipresent. Rossetti related Plato's idea of the Good to the Tractarian belief in Christ's goodness. When Rossetti says "The old thorn shall grow out of the old stem, / And morning shall be cold and twilight grey," she is referring to the idea that there is "nothing new under the sun" and therefore no growth, no rebirth, no truth from the light of the son if one looks with the bodily eye. The physical world should only be viewed through the in-sight of "the eye of the mind." The Tractarian belief that nature is a go-between for man and God, revealing the importance of the immutability of heaven through nature's constancy. The "True Vine" is an image that emphasizes the connection between Christ and nature as ambassadors between mankind and God.

"A Portrait," written in November of 1850 according to William Rossetti (286), reflects Christina Rossetti's fixation on "eyes wide shut":

I
She gave up beauty in her tender youth,
  Gave up all hope and joy and pleasant ways;
  She covered up her eyes lest they should gaze
On vanity and chose the bitter truth.
Harsh towards herself, towards others full of ruth,
  Servant of servants, little known to praise,
  Long prayers and fasts trenched on her nights and days:
She schooled herself to sights and sounds uncouth
That with the poor and stricken she might make
  A home, until the least of all sufficed
Her wants; her own self learned she to forsake,
Counting all earthly gain but hurt and loss.
So with calm will she choose and bore the cross

And hated all for love of Jesus Christ.

II
They knelt in silent anguish by her bed,
  And could not weep; but calmly there she lay.
  All pain had left her; and the sun's last ray
Shone through upon her, warming into red
The shady curtains. In her heart she said:
  "Heaven opens; I leave these and go away;
  The Bridegroom calls,--shall the Bride seek to stay?"
Then low upon her breast she bowed her head.
O lily flower, O gem of priceless worth,
  O dove with patient voice and patient eyes,
  O fruitful vine amid a land of dearth,
    O maid replete with loving purities,
Thou bowedst down thy head with friends on earth
  To raise it with the saints in Paradise. (Crump 1, 122)

    In this poem, Rossetti begins to develop her concept that all women should avoid using the "eye" to perceive the world of vanity, "the land of dearth," which corrupts the "I." The female "portrait" in this poem is connected to Mary (the second Eve), to the Holy Spirit, and to Christ with the words "lily," "dove", and "fruitful vine." This poem blends Pre-Raphaelite and Tractarian beliefs as it uses the image of Christ as the ultimate bridegroom (Lo Tempio 144). Medieval Christian imagery impacted Pre-Raphaelite philosophy; the concept of Christ as bridegroom comes from the medieval metaphor that Mary's womb was a tabernacle where God wed humanity, as Gail McMurray Gibson ponders (138, 173). Christina Rossetti, who turned down suitors but also rejected the sisterhood due to personal incompatibility, saw her love as ultimately fulfilled by Christ's love. She did not want to experience God as the Bible said through her earthbound husband or from anything associated with the sensual world that the bodily "eye" fixates on. Instead, the figure in the poem tries to see Christ in the least of God's creations, in the poor and unfortunate, waiting for rebirth in the afterlife. When dying, the figure in the poem gains insight. She sees this insight as a "gem of priceless worth," something that has value beyond the temporal worldly gains. In-sight should always be the object of the gaze, not the material world of vanity.

"She gave up beauty in her tender youth," the first line of stanza I of "A Portrait," is an example of the Pre-Raphaelite adherence to Ruskin's definition of Typical Beauty which reflects the mutable world. The Pre-Raphaelite predilection towards Biblical imagery, the story of the Bride and Bridegroom related to Christ and his followers, and the illuminative use of light in "the sun's last ray/Shone through her, warming into red/The shady curtains" (II, ll. 3-5) are qualities of Pre-Raphaelite painting. Christina Rossetti believed that illumination came from "the third eye," a vision in the poem that sees the rewards of heaven that those who surround the figure on the deathbed cannot bear witness to. The bride and bridegroom, a reflection of our first parents, is often used in the New Testament and is included in this poem to reveal the speaker's relationship with God in death.

Also reflective of Pre-Raphaelite art is the melancholy tone as in the lines "chose the bitter truth./Harsh towards herself, towards others full of ruth" (I, ll. 4-5). This attitude evolves into a demonstration of medieval feminine charity where the central figure in the poem ministered to "poor and stricken" (I, l. 9) until she "raised [her] head with the saints in Paradise" (II, l. 14). The figure can "see" Christ's teachings in the lowly and forlorn. Another Pre-Raphaelite influence is the picture of nature reflecting the transcendence of Christ in heaven as in the last six lines of the poem. Later in Christina Rossetti's life, her "Eve" poetry will reflect these attitudes concerning humility and chastity in the world of vanity as first pondered by her in her early poetry.

Another poem which reflects the skepticism of worldly vanities is "A Fair World Though a Fallen" written on August 30, 1851 according to William Rossetti (303):

> You tell me that the world is fair in spite
>   Of the old Fall; and that I should not turn
>   So to the grave, and let my spirit yearn
> After the quiet of the long last night.
> Have I then shut mine eyes against the light,
>   Grief-deafened lest my spirit should discern?
>   Yet how could I keep silence when I burn?
> And who can give me comfort?--Hear the right.
> Have patience with the weak and sick at heart:
> Bind up the wounded with a tender touch,
> Comfort the sad, tear-blinded as they go:--
> For, though I failed to choose the better part,

> Were it a less unutterable woe
> If we should come to love this world too much?
>
> (Rossetti, William 302).

The belief in ministering to mankind from the Tractarian tenets is present in this poem. The concern displayed in *Goblin Market* for allowing the eye to absorb too much of the world of vanity as Laura does, which is her downfall, is reflected in this poem also. This is Eve's problem as well. The fair world is really a world of shadows, like those in Plato's "Allegory of the Cave," shadows of "unutterable woe," of those who are "wounded" and "sick of heart." By loving "this world too much," one shuts one's eye of the mind to the light. The eye in this poem should only absorb God's "light" that comes from the "eye of the mind"; this insight leads the figure in the poem to nurture those in need through charity towards "the weak and sick at heart" (ll. 5 and 9).

The light from "the eye of the mind" nurtures the soul; this is turn helps those who truly "see" to nurture those around them, to lead those around them to Plato's idea of "The Good." Christ is the illumination source for the Good, for growth and nourishment. Although the world is fallen, insight coming from in-sight still reflects God's "comfort" (ll. 2 and 8).

The love relationship between the repentant and Christ, an important tenet of the Oxford Movement, is apparent in many of Christina Rossetti's poems including "A Bruised Reed Shall He Not Break." "Thy will at least to love, that burns within/And thirsteth after Me" (ll. 3 and 4). In Plato's "Allegory of the Cave," the sun burns the sight of the person who has been in the cave only seeing shadows of reality. The love of the "son" is what Rossetti interprets as Plato's idea of the Truth. People "thirst" for knowledge of the private gaze. The eye operates best when being illuminated by God's love. This "thirst," the void left by the absence of Christ's love, is found also in Rossetti's poems "The Convent Threshold" and "Echo."

She speaks of this in the last stanza of "The Convent Threshold" and in the second stanza of "Echo" written in 1854 as William Rossetti indicates (314). The "yearning eyes" (Crump 1, 61, l. 75) in "The Convent Threshold" and the "thirsting longing eyes"(Crump 1, 46, l. 10) in "Echo" represent the void in the souls of women caused by viewing and desiring the temptations of the material world which is a fall from grace. This emptiness can only be filled by focusing on the in-sight of the "minds' eye." "Memory," published in November 1857 (Rossetti, William 334) and the poem

"L.E.L." which, according to William Rossetti, was published in February 1859 (345) echo the themes of the loneliness and emptiness of the material world.

The poem "Echo" also examines the end of human misery; desire, associated with the public gaze on the material world, ends when the body dies and is replaced by the longing to look upon The Good. "Oh harps, oh crowns of plenteous stars,/Oh green palm branches many-leaved--Eye hath not seen, nor ear hath heard,/Nor heart conceived" is another poetic creation that illustrates the loss of desire in the poem "Paradise," published in February 1854 as William Rossetti asserts (181). The "eye hath not seen" what the "eye of the mind" can reveal.

In Christina Rossetti's poem "Listening" written in 1854 as William Rossetti explains (313), she reveals that a woman should not fixate on what "men would reckon fair" but on what Christ, the bough and vine in the poem, reveals an the enlightened path:

>She listened like a cushat dove
>   That listens to its mate alone:
>She listened like a cushat dove
>   That love but only one.
>
>Not fair as men would reckon fair,
>Nor noble as they count the line:
>
>Only as graceful as a bough,
>   And tendrils of the vine:
>Only as noble as sweet Eve
>   Your ancestress and mine.
>
>And downcast were her dovelike eyes
>And downcast was her tender cheek;
>Her pulses fluttered like a dove
>   To hear him speak. (Rossetti, William 313)

Christ is the living vine to Tractarians; this concept of the living, fruitful vine connects Christ to all daughters of Eve and recurs often in Christina Rossetti's poetry. The penitent look upon the face of Christ through in-sight; Christ is depicted as a lover in the poem. The penitent have downcast eyes, humbled in the presence of spiritual rather than earthly "nobility." Christ is the "sun," the source of enlightenment. The world of men is a world of falsehood and illusion. Although most people would see the world of commerce and family life as the "real" world, this world is a world of shadows to Rossetti. The "real" world is the afterlife.

The poem "The World" adds another dimension to her poetic exploration and is a landmark poem in Rossetti's development of her concept of "the eye of the mind." "The World," a sonnet written in June of 1854 as William Rossetti observes (182), presents a metaphor of the world as a seductive temptress of material decay in juxtaposition to the description of the strength and wisdom gained from "the eye of the mind" discussed in Rossetti's other poems.

> By day she wooes me, soft, exceeding fair:
> But all night as the moon so changeth she;
> Loathsome and foul with hideous leprosy
> And subtle serpents gliding in her hair.
> By day she wooes me to the outer air,
> Ripe fruit, sweet flower, and full satiety:
> But through the night, a beast she grins at me,
> A very monster void of love and prayer.
> By day she stands a lie: by night she stands
> In all the naked horror of the truth
> With pushing horns and clawed and clutching hands.
> Is this a friend indeed; that I should sell
> My soul to her, give her my life and youth,
> Till my feet, cloven too, take hold on hell? (Crump 1, 76)

In "The World," the world is envisioned as a woman, one who is "a very monster void of love and prayer" and one "with pushing horns and clawed and clutching hands" (ll. 8 and 11). This description sounds very much like Milton's characteristics of the monstrous mother, Sin, in *Paradise Lost*. This delineation is also reminiscent of the characterization of the corrupted Laura and the goblin men in *Goblin Market*. Rossetti says that she will not "sell [her] soul to her" (l. 13), a concept that will be fully developed in *Goblin Market* where Laura sells her soul for the goblin men's wares, which can be compared here to the world's "ripe fruit" and "full satiety" (l. 6). This concept is related to Eve, who sold her soul to Satan for the forbidden fruit in Eden. If one does not gain insight from "the eye of the mind," one does not grow but withers. The object of the gaze should never be the material world of corruption.

The vanities of the public gaze are examined again in "The World" and compared to Eve's "lost garden Paradise." The public gaze versus in-sight is also examined in "An After-Thought," published in December 1855 according to William Rossetti (319). Tractarian absorption with the afterlife, not with the world of vanity, is apparent in "An After-Thought" in the lines "Oh come the day of death, that day/Of rest which cannot pass away!/When the last work is wrought,the last/Pang of pain is felt and past,/And the blessed door made fast" (ll. 63-8). The blessed door can be interpreted here as the physical eyes which are shut forever in death, in other word "made fast." Nothing but the "eye of the mind" remains, forever looking on the paradise of the sun/son rather than on the worldly vanities of "pain."

Central to Christina Rossetti's poetry on in-sight are concepts presented in "A Better Resurrection" from June of 1857, as William Rossetti indicates (192):

> I have no wit, no words, no tears;
>   My heart within me like a stone
> Is numbed too much for hopes or fears;
>   Look right, look left, I dwell alone;
> I lift mine eyes, but dimmed with grief
>   No everlasting hills I see;
> My life is in the falling leaf.
>   O Jesus, quicken me.
>
> My life is like a faded leaf,
>   My harvest dwindled to a husk;
> Truly my life is void and brief
>   And tedious in the barren dusk;
> My life is like a frozen thing,
>   No bud nor greenness can I see:
> Yet rise it shall--the sap of Spring;
>   O Jesus, rise in me.
>
> My life is like a broken bowl,

> A broken bowl that cannot hold
> One drop of water for my soul
>   Or cordial in the searching cold;
> Cast in the fire the perished thing,
>   Melt and remould it, till it be
> A royal cup for Him my King:
>   O Jesus, drink of me. (Crump I 68)

I believe Christina Rossetti believed "eyes wide shut" was the "better resurrection"; in other words, in death, the physical eyes are permanently closed and cannot look on the outer world. Therefore, in death, the inner eye is what remains wide open, seeing the "real" world of being with Christ in the afterlife. When looking "right" and "left," all the narrator of the poem sees in the world of sin and depravity, the world of despairing vanity. This world is a world of aloneness. The world viewed in the "eye of the mind" is a world of solidarity, of union with those who are also redeemed by Christ's insight. If one lifts one's eyes, one only sees the sky. To find the nourishment of "The Good," one must look within. The Good is the object of the gaze. Lifting one's eyes is looking in the wrong place; it makes one even more grief-stricken. Life is "like a faded leaf," "void and brief and tedious" and frozen without the sight of the mind's eye which is the nourishing, rejuvenating water for the soul.

The stanza on the "broken bowl" is about the sensual world. Feasting, related to the garden of Eden, is a fall from innocence. The restoration of purity only comes from in-sight. The original fall from innocence (the broken bowl) and the worldly temptations created from that fall are redeemed by the icon of the Holy Grail, the cup of Christ's mercy. This cup of mercy is the true nourishment that one receives through in-sight. The different realities, the material world of illusions versus the world of the sun/son, are represented in the form of the "broken bowl"; Rossetti believes that only by rejecting the world of shadows and turning towards the true light can a person fuse the parts of the broken bowl into a different kind of bowl, a different kind of consumption, a consumption of that which only the eye of the mind can reveal.

This theme is also addressed in the poem *Goblin Market* where Rossetti struggles to fuse the twin natures of Laura and Lizzie together. Laura represents those who look on and lust for vanity in the material world, and Lizzie is the symbol of insight as she stands with eyes shut confronting the goblin men. To consume knowledge and wisdom through in-sight, one must block out worldly desires and concentrate on the private gaze.

In the poem "A Birthday" (Crump 1, 36), Rossetti discusses how finding The Good from in-sight is like a birthday, another type of resurrection, to the poem's narrator. The peacock's eyes (l. 12), which also appear in Rossetti's poem, "Bird or Beast?" represent God's omnipresence in the material world. These eyes also symbolize the soul tainted by the temptations of the world of vanity.

In Christina Rossetti's poem "Mary Magadalene" written in February of 1846, as William Rossetti observes (89), Mary Magdalene silently approaches "Trembling betwixt hope and fear,/She sought the King of Heaven,/Forsook the evil of her ways,/Loved much, and was forgiven" (ll. 17-20). Here "deep repentance" (l. 1) saves her. Repentance to Rossetti indicated that the redeemed individual had turned away from the sensual world (in the case of Magdalene, this was a world of prostitution) and sought The Good.

The imagery of the fallen who turn away from the world of vanity and embrace in-sight is reinforced in the first four stanzas of the poem "The Martyr," published in May 1846 according to William Rossetti (92), where reference is made to a woman ensnared by the emptiness of her fallen state who wants to "win a crown" (l. 12) through repentance and leave life's prison.

>   SEE, the sun hath risen--
>   Lead her from the prison;
> She is young and tender,--lead her tenderly:
>   May no fear subdue her,
>   Lest the saints be fewer--
> Lest her place in heaven be lost eternally.
>
>   Forth she came, not trembling,
>   No nor yet dissembling
> An o'erwhelming terror weighing her down, down;
>   Little, little heeding
>   Earth, but only pleading
> For the strength to triumph and to win a crown.
>
>   All her might was rallied

>   To her heart; not pallid
> Was her cheek, but glowing with a glorious red;
>   Glorious red and saintly,
>   Never paling faintly,
> But still flushing, kindling still, without thought of dread.
>
>   On she went, on faster,
>   Trusting in her Master,
> Feeling that His eye watched o'er her lovingly;
>   He would prove and try her,
>   But would not deny her
> When her soul had past, for His sake, patiently. (Crump 1, 91).

The first few lines of the first stanza of this poem clearly reflect "The Allegory of the Cave." The first word is "SEE" written in capital letters. Seeing has nothing to do with the physical eye that absorbs only the illusionary world of vanity. To truly "SEE," the seer must be released, like the figure in "The Allegory of the Cave" from "Life's prison." "Life's prison" is the shadows on the walls, the world of the senses that must be shunned so that the world of in-sight, the true object of the gaze, can be revealed. To be released from "life's prison," also means to die and forsake the material world for the world of The Good. The sun/son leads the narrative figure toward the true light and away from the shadows. A person's place in heaven is lost forever if the person does not learn to "SEE." To "SEE," the person cannot heed the earth. Seeing is frightening just as the individual who is freed from the ties that bind in the cave and is allowed to reach the surface to gaze upon the sun for the first time trembles in fear. Christ's eyes are the eyes of the Master. These eyes are the eyes of the sun/son, and those who look with the mind's eye upon The Good gain knowledge and wisdom. These concepts are reiterated in Christina Rossetti's poem "Sweet Death," published in February 1849 as William Rossetti discusses (117), where young blossoms and beauty die but the God of truth is the "full harvest" (Crump I, 74, l. 23). Nature is mutable, but the "full harvest" for Rossetti was growth and nourishment received by focusing on the mind's eye.

Another poem with a similar theme is "The Bourne," published in February 1854 as William Rossetti claims (311). In "The Bourne," a poem about death and burial, Rossetti once again reveals the emptiness of worldly vanity.

>   Underneath the growing grass,

> Underneath the living flowers,
> Deeper than the sound of showers:
> There we shall not count the hours
> By the shadows as they pass.
>
> Youth and health will be but vain,
> Beauty reckoned of no worth:
> There a very little girth
>
> Can hold round what once the earth
> Seemed too narrow to contain. (Crump 1, 142).

The shadows of the grass and flowers, like the shadows interpreted by the prisoners in Plato's allegory, should not be the focus of attention, should not be the place where we should "count the hours." The eye, "a very little girth," cannot behold what is "too narrow" for the earth to contain, that being the inspiration of in-sight. The world is too narrow to hold all that The Good encompasses. Published in January 1856 as William Rossetti articulates (321), Christina Rossetti's poem "Shut Out" discusses the "shadowless spirit" (Crump 1, 156). The spirit is revealed by viewing the sun/son. It is a shadowless place, away from the darkness of Plato's cave in his allegory.

Many of Rossetti's "seasonal cycle" poems including "Winter: My Secret" written in November of 1857 (Rossetti, William 336) explore the empty, fallen world that the eyes behold and the re-membering of the world that only the eye of the mind can envision. Human beings must not put too much "trust" (Crump 1, 47, l. 23) in the seasonal cycle because the physical world is the site of temptation. Faith must be placed in God/The Good alone.

It is apparent in Rossetti's poetry that she was fascinated with Plato's theory about "the eye of the mind" and used her own interpretation of Plato's allegory in her writing. Kooistra discusses that Rossetti sold some of her poetry, namely the poems "Christmas Carols" and "A Heavenly Chime," to the aptly-named Boston periodical *Wide Awake*, which seems to be an ironic and perhaps purposeful publishing collaboration, since Rossetti's writing is burgeoning with symbolic references to eyes open and eyes closed (Kooistra, *Christina Rossetti and Illustration* 34), and in my opinion, "eyes wide shut" as this chapter has illustrated.

Christina Rossetti was not only obsessed with the gaze and the object of the gaze in her writing from the perspective of Plato's "Allegory of the Cave," but she also re-fashioned John Milton's Eve from *Paradise Lost* into Rossetti's own vision of Eve and the creation cycle in Rossetti's poetry and prose. Chapter 2 is a feminist interrogation of Rossetti's writing concerning her re-figurement of Eve.

CHAPTER 2

Re-configuring Eve – Christina Rossetti's Reaction to John Milton's *Paradise Lost* in Rossetti's Poetry and Prose

Christina Rossetti's poem "Eve," written on January 30, 1865, reflects decades of work during which Rossetti pondered Eve's influence on female identity, as William Rossetti indicates (374). In this poem, Christina Rossetti reflects upon the shadow that the original sin of Eve placed on the women of the world. In the first four stanzas, Rossetti reveals a very different version of Eve's character than appears in John Milton's epic poem *Paradise Lost*.

'While I sit at the door,
  Sick to gaze within,
Mine eye weepeth sore
For sorrow and sin:
As a tree my sin stands
To darken all lands;
Death is the fruit it bore.

'How have Eden bowers grown
Without Adam to bend them?
How have Eden flowers blown,
Squandering their sweet breath,
Without me to tend them?
The Tree of Life was ours,
Tree twelvefold-fruited,
Most lofty tree that flowers,
Most deeply rooted:
I chose the Tree of Death.

'Hadst thou but said me nay,
  Adam my brother,
I might have pined away--

47

> I, but none other:
> God might have let thee stay
> Safe in our garden,
> By putting me away
> Beyond all pardon.
>
> 'I, Eve, sad mother
> Of all who must live,
> I, not another,
> Plucked bitterest fruit to give
> My friend, husband, lover.
> O wanton eyes, run over!
> Who but I should grieve?
> Cain hath slain his brother:
> Of all who must die mother,
> Miserable Eve!' (Crump 1, 156)

The concept of a man as friend/husband/lover (which is the way Rossetti views her relationship with God), the expression of cyclic imagery, the hope of redemption reflected in nature's munificence, the use of personal and simple authorial tone (versus John Milton's sense of sublime epic): all of these are distinctly Christina Rossetti's depiction of Eve. Unlike Dinah Roe who asserts that Rossetti's Eve poetry is "characterized by confusion and ambivalence," I believe Rossetti's writings concerning Eve are purposeful and focused.

Rossetti's depiction of Eve was an obvious deconstruction of the portrait of Eve in *Paradise Lost*. There was a wide variety of reactions to John Milton and his poetry during the Victorian period, and this reveals Milton's great influence on the age. For the most part, John Milton's works were revered by the Victorians. However, the Tories, High Churchmen, Catholics, Tractarians, and Pre-Raphaelites, with whom Christina Rossetti aligned her philosophy, reacted to Milton's *Paradise Lost* with disapproval, as James Nelson observes (12). John Keble and John Henry Newman of the Oxford Movement found some of Milton's works disappointing even though they admired his sonnet technique, and Christina Rossetti echoed this impression (12). This element of the religious community felt that Milton had placed too much emphasis in *Paradise*

Lost on the heroism and nobility of characters like Satan and the fallen angels, who should have been portrayed as foul and wicked (Nelson 89).

In view of Milton's vast influence on the Victorians, it is not surprising that Christina Rossetti had her own opinion of Milton's works. In an unpublished letter to Sir Wyndham Dunstan, F.R.S., written in May 1894, Christina Rossetti asserted, "Milton I cannot warm towards, even let alone all theological questions," as Dorothy Stuart indicates (106). Rossetti died in December of this same year; even at the very end of her life, she still found Milton's works wanting. Milton's *Paradise Lost* and *Paradise Regained* attempted to answer the question of human destiny and the human condition as Christian Rossetti's religious poetry did, but Christina Rossetti felt that Milton had missed the mark by creating an account of the fall of man that did not emphasize enough the most important aspect--woman's paramount place in the action. This attitude reflects Christina Rossetti's Tractarian influence. Milton's work emphasizes the fall of Satan and Adam with not enough emphasis on the role of woman (Eve, Mary) in the heavenly universe.

This chapter explores those aspects of Christina Rossetti's life and works, primarily her prose works, which define her displeasure with John Milton's *Paradise Lost*, specifically his depiction of Eve. Christina Rossetti's works speak to the idea that Milton does not do enough to liberate Eve in his epic poem. Rossetti agreed with some Victorian critics who saw Milton's authorship of Eve in *Paradise Lost* and *Paradise Regained* as an assumption "that his theological position was the ultimate one," as Nelson explains (29). According to Tractarian philosophy, Milton's version and even the Bible's story from Genesis "was not adequate to explain rationally or justify sufficiently the ways of God to man[kind]" (133).

Christina Rossetti's sense of self as daughter, as potential wife and mother, and as woman was linked to her self-definition as "literary creature/creator." From Rossetti's perspective, women were all daughters of Eve. Central to this idea is the concept of the creation/redemption cycle. It is a cycle because God created Eve who is the mother of mankind, the Virgin Mary brought Christ into the world, and Christ is part of the Godhead who created Eve. In other words, God creates Eve but, as the mother of mankind, Eve ultimately creates God, made man in Christ. All women contribute to this cycle of creation and redemption by being a creator in some form, either as an artist or as a procreator.

Christina Rossetti emphasizes her relationship as a daughter of Eve, who figuratively eats from the tree of Good and Evil to gain knowledge, as a means of not submitting to past literary canon, according to Sandra Gilbert and Susan Gubar (220). This is a revision of Milton's works, not a subversive act towards God, whom Christina Rossetti revered and to whom Rossetti dedicated much of her poetry. Therefore, Christina Rossetti's muse is God, the parallel to Milton's use of the mythic muse Urania in *Paradise Lost*. Christina Rossetti rewrites/recreates *Paradise Lost* in her own works "so as to make it a more accurate mirror of female experience" (Gilbert and Gubar 220). In the work *Goblin Market* in particular, she reacts to Milton's epic work by creating her own myth as an "encoded artwork, concealing female secrets within male-devised genres and conventions" (220). Her later poetry and prose on the subject of Eve expand on what she originally contemplates about Eve in her early poetry and in *Goblin Market*.

Milton's Influence

Rossetti's Eve, a personae she developed over decades of writing, is a reworking of Milton's version of Eve. To most Victorians, however, Milton was a saint and his "poems were memorized and treasured," as Nelson observes (4). Particular to give homage to Milton were the Whigs, Evangelicals, and dissenters in Victorian society (11). Poets in the 19th century like Hazlitt, Keats, Shelley, Wordsworth, and Blake praised Milton's technical poetic prowess; critics of this time also admired his progressive democratic attitudes on political, moral, and social issues.

T.B. Macaulay is a representative of the early Victorian critical voice concerning Milton's place in literary posterity. Macaulay asserts that John Milton's works can be "classed among the noblest productions of the human mind" (qtd in Smith, Herbert 4). As James Thorpe points out, in 1888, Matthew Arnold praised "the power of Milton's art" (374) "Milton has made the great style no longer an exotic here; he has made it an inmate amongst us [the English-speaking populace], a leaven, and a power" (376).

Ralph Waldo Emerson wrote in 1838 that Milton's forte was his ability to inspire his readership. "Are not all men fortified by the remembrance of the bravery, the purity, the temperance, the toil, the independence and the angelic devotion of this man, who, in a revolutionary age, taking counsel only of himself, endeavored, in his writings and in his life, to carry out the life of a man to new heights of spiritual grace and dignity, without any abatement of its strength?" (Thorpe 367). Samuel Taylor

Coleridge in 1818 commended Milton's recognition of Adam and Eve's "mutual rationality" and spiritual equality in *Paradise Lost*, as Thorpe asserts (96).

Mary Wollstonecraft, writing in the 1790's, would have agreed with Coleridge's viewpoint on Milton. In her time, Milton was viewed by women like Charlotte Smith, Catherine Talbot, and Anna Barbauld as an anarchist inciting women to rebel against their suppressed state, as Joseph Wittreich illustrates (6). Wollstonecraft also saw that Milton's Eve was "one of the masculine stereotypes of female nature" and revealed more about the male imagination in Renaissance England and their view of woman as the Puritan housewife than about the Bible (13). Wollstonecraft believed Milton was attempting in *Paradise Lost* to condemn such behavior by men. "For Milton, a woman was not a mere satellite" (13). Wollstonecraft commended Milton's attempts in his epic poem to try to free women of the "bondage of species," to attempt to show women as the social and cultural equals of men, but she also felt that Milton's attempts were not nearly persuasive enough to counteract years of patriarchal oppression.

Depiction of Eve in *Paradise Lost*

Milton's Eve is a complex portrait based on the sources of Genesis, Anderini's *L'Adama*, Peyton's *Glass of Tome*, and Beaumont's *Psyche*, as Dudley Hutcherson indicates (28). Eve is inferior in the hierarchal structure, but the harmony in Eden, the mutual respect, loyalty and obligation, is emphasized just as much as the hierarchy. An example of this is in Book 4 where Milton describes "our two first Parents" as "Two of far nobler shape erect and tall,/Godlike erect, with native Honour clad/In naked Majestie seemd Lords of all,/ And worthie seemd,/for in thir looks Divine/The image of thir glorious Maker shon," (ll. 288-92, Shawcross *The Complete Poetry of John Milton* 324). This description of Adam and Eve is equal; it indicates no superiority in delineating Adam.

Milton's syntax is not derogatory toward Eve but embodies the mutual need between the sexes. Eve is defined in Book 8 not in subordinate terms but as "societie" and "companie" for Adam (ll. 444-51). Barbara K. Lewalski asserts that the interdependence and powerful bonding of Adam and Eve reveals Milton's complex treatment of women in his poem (11). Eve participates in Milton's Eden in the full range of human activities; Milton paints her with qualities that are exceptional for his time. Adam and Eve are both held individually responsible for their actions. However,

Lewalski agrees with other feminists who believe that Milton does not go far enough with his depiction of gender reciprocity.

Pre-Raphaelite and Tractarian Reactions to Milton

Milton's name was not revered by the supporters of the Pre-Raphaelite Movement including Dante Gabriel Rossetti and Christina Rossetti, whose interest in medievalism and the joy of art as it reveals the sacramental aesthetic ran contrary to their view of Milton as the stern, ascetic Puritan, as Bump asserts (324). The followers of the Pre-Raphaelite Movement were disapproving of classical and mythological allusion when mixed with orthodox Christian iconography. Eve is compared to the classical image of Sin, Satan's daughter, in *Paradise Lost*. Sin is depicted as female and serpentine like Satan (Gilbert and Gubar 197). Sin is described as the essence of monstrous maternity, paralleled with Eve's fall as the catalyst for her "slave[ry] to the species" (198). Sin is vulnerable to the charms of Satan, opening the gates of Hell in disobedience to God's edict, just as Eve disobeys God's commandment and succumbs to Satan's trickery. Christina Rossetti found this connection between Sin and Eve in Milton's work to be a misinterpretation of the female role in God's plan.

Paradise Lost was primarily admired by the Victorians for its "sublimity"; this aspect of Milton's epic work the Tractarians looked on with disapproval, as Nelson argues (40). Some of the Victorian artists and poets were inspired by Milton to "cram their works with enormous objects and panoramas, limitless space, vast irregular landscapes, titanic beings, and cataclysmic occurrences" (Nelson 44). In contrast, the works of Christina Rossetti, Charlotte Bronte, and Gerard Manley Hopkins from the 1800's use religious themes that deal with the private, personal, and singular experience and with the religious communal network much like Dante's *Divine Comedy*.

John Ruskin and John Henry Newman felt that simple plainness and purity was best suited to Bible stories like the teachings of Christ (89). They also felt Milton's emphasis on the nobility of Satan and the fallen angels to be inappropriate. As a true Tractarian, Christina Rossetti would have seen this focus on the rebellious fallen angels and on Adam as skewed and sacrilegious; the Church of England abhorred idol worship. Christ as the Almighty, the descendant of Eve, was the only appropriate subject of worship and therefore should have been the central focus in *Paradise Lost*, according to David LoTempio (37).

Reserve is another important aspect to Tractarian aesthetics. Part of this reserve required that the disciples of God await the unfolding of God's plan with patience; to try to comprehend the entirety of God or to believe this is possible is the folly of pride. This would be another objection the Tractarians would have to Milton's *Paradise Lost*. Milton attempts to explain God's motives and plan. Another aspect of Milton's Puritan tendencies is the Puritan view of imagination. The Puritans saw imagination as the culprit to man's temptation and fall which is outlined in Milton's portrayal of Eve in *Paradise Lost*.

Female Reactions to Milton

Milton's position of honor in the literary canon had a great impact on future generations of writers, particularly female ones. Although there are contemporary feminists like Joan Mallory Webber who believe that Milton was a "modernist" whose poem was preparing the way for feminist thinking because his poem was an appeal to the victimized, there are just as many feminist thinkers from the 19th and 20th centuries who disagree with this interpretation of Milton (Webber 6). The "politics of reading the patriarchal canon" holds up "the ideals of 'thinking like a man,'" as Anabel Patterson suggests (21). This pressures female writers, according to Elaine Showalter and Judith Fetterley, to identify with the male viewpoint or position of power against the female perspective.

Milton's depiction of the relationship between Adam and Eve reveals another important aspect in Christina Rossetti's philosophy. Adam is actually viewed by some critics as more culpable than Eve for the fall of mankind since Adam's connection to "right reason" was supposed to help him lead Eve to the path of righteousness (*Paradise Lost*, Book 12, l. 84). Therefore, Adam is seen as the greater transgressor, as Philip Gallagher interrogates (128). One place in Milton's poem where this is revealed is in Book 6, lines 908-9. Adam is instructed in this manner: "But list'n not to his Temptations, warn/Thy weaker." Some feminists would have a problem with this interpretation, but Christina Rossetti who, as a true Victorian woman, recognized a woman's inferior position to her father, brother, or husband in society, would have concurred. Christina Rossetti's difficulty sprang from the custom in Victorian society concerning marriage directly related to Milton's line in Book 4, lines 299-301 of *Paradise Lost*, "Hee for God only, shee for God in him:/ His fair large Front and Eye sublime declar'd/Absolute rule." In fact, Christina Rossetti writes about this specific passage of *Paradise Lost* in sonnet 5 of *Monna Innominata*, as Sharon Smulders ponders (133).

Another passage which pertains to this subject is in Book 4 of *Paradise Lost*, lines 635-638, where Eve addresses Adam stating, "My Author and Disposer, what thou bidst/Unargu'd I obey; so God ordains,/God is thy Law, thou mine: to know no more/Is womans happiest knowledge and her praise" (Shawcross *The Complete Poetry of John Milton* 333). Christina Rossetti found this idea of knowledge and experience of God through another agent a stifling concept. She turned down several suitors for her hand in marriage due to religious differences. It is probable that these religious differences came from her obsession with wanting to know God first hand, either through the creation of her poetry, or through acceptance of God as her husband in the vows taken as a nun. Rossetti felt her temperament was not suited to entering the convent as her sister Maria had done, but she obviously contemplated this road to closeness with God as explained in her poem "The Convent Threshold." Also, the Tractarians believed that celibacy was a legitimate alternative to marriage; living the ascetic life was promoted by believers in the Oxford Movement.

Christina Rossetti's works, especially *Goblin Market,* are viewed by many feminist critics as "revisionary critiques" of the patriarchal tenets of literary voice and of the characterizations of Eve, Satan, and Adam as depicted in *Paradise Lost* (Gilbert and Gubar 189). Christina Rossetti shared this perspective with her female predecessors and contemporaries Mary Shelley, Elizabeth Barrett Browning, and Charlotte and Emily Bronte. Christina Rossetti and other female writers of the 19th century believed in a female consciousness that was a reworking of the "cosmology" of Milton's epic poem. This idea speaks to the core of this thesis: Christina Rossetti saw the role of motherhood/the role of creator as a most significant partnership or parallel connection between woman and God that men had no claim to. As an orthodox Tractarian, Rossetti believed Eve's sin was part of a pre-ordained plan where woman ultimately participated in the redemption of mankind. A fallen woman, the mother of mankind, was the ancestor of a pure woman who brought God-made-man into the world to redeem the world's sins. The sense of female powerlessness in a patriarchal universe is undercut in Christina Rossetti's works by her devotion to God's creation cycle that only women could participate in.

ROSSETTI'S "EVE" POETRY AND PROSE

Accompanying the sense of fulfillment and redemption through creation in all of Christina Rossetti's religious poetry, and particularly in her "Eve" poetry and prose, is a deep sense of emptiness. This emptiness is created by the patriarchal vision that the stain of the orginal sin came from Eve. Male domination of women to keep order after Eve's fall also controls the image of Eve as the perpetuator of mankind's doom. This leaves women with a feeling of guilt and worthlessness, a "nothingness." The "nothingness" of female perspective in the patriarchy is made into a "somethingness," as David Willbern professes (245), by Christina Rossetti's poetry on Eve. Rossetti's own "silence and absence" definitely represent "a pregnancy" (247) to Rossetti; it symbolizes her philosophical adherence to the ascetic life which ultimately will bring forth the fruit of life everlasting with Christ.

However, the loneliness of waiting for this day is an arduous task. Because of this, Christina Rossetti takes hope in the changing seasons. The bounty of female imagery is apparent in Rossetti's poetry: her poems are saturated with the "I" and the "eye," with circles and cycles. The "eye" perceives the material world of vanity which tempts the conscience; therefore, the "eye" affects what the "I," the soul, becomes. In fact, the first person "I" appears in ninety percent of Christina Rossetti's poems. Naming or noting the "nothingness" (Willbern 249) was one of Adam and Eve's activities in Eden. The "O" is also a symbol for the word "cipher" (253) and this sense of littleness, of the triviality of life, especially for Victorian women, is at the heart of Christina Rossetti's poetry. The circular orifices of the female body are symbolized in Rossetti's works (253).

"God is a circle whose center is everywhere" (255). Eve was the mother of the human race whose Fall in Eden had started a birth series of life, death, and infinity just like "the widening circles that emanate from a single disturbance in the surface of a pond" (254). In the beginning, there was the nothingness of chaos which was filled in the end with the cage of the knowledge of good and evil.

The imagery of female nothingness is an integral part of Christina Rossetti's poetry and prose and is of paramount importance to Rossetti's creation of her poetry about Eve from 1846 to 1859 and to her later poetry and prose. Patriarchal power in a Victorian woman's life adds to the sense of female silencing which is a punishment for all women due to Eve's fall. An example of this can be found in Christina Rossetti's poem "Mary Magadalene" written in February of 1846 (Rossetti, William 89). Mary Magdalene, another fallen woman, silently comes "Trembling betwixt hope and fear,/She sought the King of Heaven,/Forsook the evil of her ways,/Loved much, and was forgiven" (ll. 17-20). Here "deep repentance" (l. 1) saves her, filling the void that fallen status creates for women. Mary Magdalene and Eve are part of a chain of sacrifice that culminates in Christ's martyrdom for the souls of the repentant.

Christina Rossetti's later poems and prose works (1860-1894) reflect an evolution of the character of Eve. Christina Rossetti began to relate the life of the fallen woman, Eve, more personally to herself and to other Victorian women in her later poetry. Eve's fall brought pain and death into the world. The silence of death is sweet but the pain of life is not; this is the key aspect to the poem, published in April 1863, "Life and Death" (Rossetti, William 359), which examines the Pre-Raphaelite view of nature reflecting heavenly transcendence as well as life's transience. A poem which expands upon these themes is "Bird or Beast?" In this poem from August of 1864 (Rossetti, William 369), Christina Rossetti uses a simplicity of tone and language admired by the Tractarians, that the presence of the "dove" and "lamb" in Eden were a warning from God concerning respect and obedience (important Tractarian tenets) after the fall.

    Did any bird come flying
     After Adam and Eve,
    When the door was shut against them
     And they sat down to grieve?

    I think not Eve's peacock
     Splendid to see,
    And I think not Adams' eagle;
     But a dove may be.

    Did any beast come pushing
     Thro' the thorny hedge
    Into the thorny thistly world
     Out from Eden's edge?

    I think not a lion
     Tho' his strength is such;
    But an innocent loving lamb

> May have done as much.
>
> If the dove preached from her bough
>   And the lamb from his sod,
> The lamb and the dove
>   Were preachers sent from God. (Crump 1, 155)

"Eve's peacock" with its feathers of many "eyes" is Rossetti's representation of the omniscience of God's presence and the vanity of the world that women must shield their eyes from if they expect to avoid a fall like Eve's. The eyes also represent the lost world of Eden and the new world of suffering. The lamb and dove represent Christ and the Holy Spirit, respectively, in Christian iconography. This poem reveals the use of nature as a go-between for man and God. Another example of nature's role as ambassador for man is found in the image of the "True Vine" which is associated to sensuality and birth in the first stanza of the poem, published in 1864, "I Know You Not" (Rossetti, William 244). It is symbolically connected to the Tree of Life in the Garden of Eden: "O Christ, the Vine with living Fruit,/The Twelvefold-fruited Tree of Life,/The Balm in Gilead after strife,/The Valley-lily and the Rose" (ll. 1-4, Rossetti, William 243). The images of the "twelvefold-fruited tree" as well as the "lily" and the "rose" appear over and over again as connections between Eve, Christ, Mary, and the sisterhood in Rossetti's "Eve" poetry.

The importance of sisterhood is expressed through the strength of creation in Rossetti's poetry. Sisterhood also fills the void in female life caused by the fall; this concept figures prominently in many of Rossetti's works. A woman's heart is related to a "stone" and to the "word" in the poem "What Would I Give?" written in 1864 (Rossetti, William 363):

> What would I give for a heart of flesh to warm me through,
> Instead of this heart of stone ice-cold whatever I do;
> Hard and cold and small, of all hearts the worst of all.
>
> What would I give for words, if only words would come;
> But now in its misery my spirit has fallen dumb:
> Oh, merry friends, go your way, I have never a word to say.

> What would I give for tears, not smiles but scalding tears,
> To wash the black mark clean, and to thaw the frost of years,
> To wash the stain ingrain and to make me clean again. (Crump 1, 142)

This poem, like "A Birthday," relates the heart of a woman, paralleled with the heartfelt guilt of Eve in the poem "Eve," to the "sacred heart" of Christ. "The black mark" or "stain" is the original sin, the fallen status of woman that can be washed clean by Christ's redemption. Human words are deficient in the place of the word of God, which fills the void of female nothingness left as a legacy to all women by Eve's fall.

"An After-Thought," published in December 1855 according to William Rossetti (319), also reveals Christina Rossetti's love of sisterhood, embodied in Eve and Rachel, who "slumber there [in heaven] forgiven," awaiting "us beneath the tress/Of Paradise, that lap of ease: They wait for us, till God shall please" (ll. 60-3). The "utter ruinous fall," the "bitter fall," of Eve, like the fall of all women, is juxtaposed to God's heavenly reward for the penitent (ll. 18 and 26). What is it that the "Angels could not strip her [Eve] of"? (l. 34). "Yet the accustomed hand for leading,/yet the accustomed heart for love: Sure she kept one part of Eden" (ll. 30-4). All women are connected by their ability to lead and love mankind in God's ways because women are the daughters of Eve; this is Eve's legacy to future generations of women.

Another significant poem concerning figurative and literal sisterhood is "The Convent Threshold." "The Convent Threshold," written in July of 1858 as William Rossetti professes (342), holds a power over the author that fills the void left in the poem "The World." The line "There's blood between us, love, my love" opens "The Convent Threshold." The "blood between us" reveals the speaker's renouncement of her bonds to her lover and to the material world in favor of the sisterhood. There is also the blood of Christ made man which bonds the blood of the family of man and the family of the sisterhood. In addition, there is the blood of the female cycle which ties all women to each other and to the birth of Christ. This ties all women to Mary, the second Eve, and to Eve, the mother of mankind. The "father's blood...[and] brother's blood" is "a bar I cannot pass" (Crump 1, 61, ll. 2 and 3). The blood which binds the patriarchy is not part of Rossetti's existence; she belongs to the "blood" of the sisterhood. Hope and guilt, referred to in "The Convent Threshold," are qualities Christina Rossetti related to Eve in her later poems and to all fallen and redeemed women after Eve. The "sinking heart" from "Vanity of Vanities" is "stained" and "soiled" in "The Convent Threshold" with the corruption of the worldly vision of "love" (ll. 7, 10, 12). Procreative love takes on an incestuous overtone since all men and women are brothers and sisters.

In "The Convent Threshold," attaining heaven's graces will "wash the spot" (l. 14), the site of fallen status brought upon women originally by Eve. The righteous who "sleep at ease among their trees,/Or wake to sing a cadence hymn with Cherubim and Seraphim" in heavenly paradise "bore the Cross" and were "racked, roasted, crushed, wrenched limb from limb" (ll. 22-6) by earthly desires. Women also bear the cross due to patriarchal oppression; their belief in sisterhood saved them. When women repent the "pleasant sin," (l. 51) their fallen status in God's kingdom, they will "rest in paradise" (l. 69) and take their rightful place next to Eve and Mary Magdalene, who followed the precept presented here by Rossetti to "repent and purge your soul and save"
(l. 81).

Another kind of nothingness, the emptiness of vanity, is the central theme in "Beauty is Vain," published in 1864 (Rossetti, William 363). This poem also is concerned with the presence of death, that "shadow" which always walks with the living.

>While roses are so red,
>   While lilies are so white
>Shall a woman exalt her face
>   Because it gives delight?
>She's not so sweet as a rose,
>   A lily's straighter than she,
>And if she were as red or white
>   She'd be but one of three.

>Whether she flush in love's summer
>   Or in its winter grow pale,
>Whether she flaunt her beauty
>   Or hide it away in a veil,
>Be she red or white,
>   And stand she erect or bowed,
>Time will win the race he runs with her

59

And hide her away in a shroud. (Crump 1, 139)

This poem reveals the vanity of beauty, the beauty of Dante's Beatrice or the loveliness of Eve as she spies her image in the pool in the garden of Eden, described in Milton's *Paradise Lost* (Book 4, ll. 455-80, Shawcross *The Complete Poetry of John Milton* 328). Female beauty is part of the vanity of the world that the Tractarians were ever-conscious of. The lily representing Christ's mother Mary and virginity which is lost in "love's summer" is related to birth and death, beauty and aging in this poem.

Many of Rossetti's poems, like "A Better Resurrection," have a religious, hymn-like quality reflecting the influence of Rossetti's Tractarian faith. The Tractarian respect for and Dantesque concept of simplicity and plainness is revealed in Rossetti's use of the images of the stone, leaf, and bowl to reveal deeper messages concerning faith. Christ's love relationship with repenting sinners, a twist on the eucharistic theme where the sinner consumes the body and blood of Christ, is revealed in "O Jesus, drink of me" (l. 24). This also relates to the Pre-Raphaelite concern with medieval iconography. The metaphor of the believer drinking from the breast of Christ, where Christ represents the mother of God's flock, was an image known by Christians from the middle ages, as Margery Kempe indicates (52). In Rossetti's poem, Christ is asked to reciprocate, to drink from the breasts of the daughters of Eve. By doing so, Christ in the poem completes the creation cycle, drinking from the breasts of the daughters of Eve, Christ's and humanities descendants. God creates Eve, the original mother, who then creates humankind; Mary, the second Eve, is one of the descendants of Eve. Through God's inspiration, Mary creates Christ who not only suckles from Mary's breast but also nourishes the rest of mankind in Rossetti's poem by suckling from the breasts of Eve and Mary's female descendants. Christ is nourished by humankind and in turn is the nourisher of humankind through his crucifixion and ressurection. Christ is the son of God. A variation of this theme of the faithful nourishing the fallen will be used later in *Goblin Market*.

A life of celibacy, honored just as much as the married life by the Tractarian faith, is another part of "A Better Resurrection," revealed in the imagery of the words "void," "barren," "frozen," "searching cold." Nature, represented by "a faded leaf" versus "the sap of Spring," reveals the transience of the world versus the eternal beauty of heaven's rewards (ll. 9 and 15). Christina Rossetti's poems and prose about Eve, written near the end of her literary career, reflect her poetic experimentation here with Tractarian doctrine including the concepts of simplicity of imagery, respect and adherence to God's laws, love between Christ and the postulant, nature as a reflection of heaven on earth, and faith in the afterlife, not in the world's vanities.

The healing power of Christ which overcomes life's vanities and man's betrayal is once more echoed in "Twice." In stanzas four, five, and six of this poem written in 1864, according to William Rossetti (367), Christina Rossetti symbolically expresses Eve's betrayal by Adam and the rejuvenation of her love by God where all fallen women's hearts, broken by man, are healed by God.

>I take my heart in my hand,
>   O my God, O my God,
>My broken heart in my hand:
>   Thou hast seen, judge Thou.
>My hope was written on sand,
>   O my God, O my God.
>Now let Thy Judgement stand--
>   Yea, judge me now.
>
>This contemned of a man,
>   This marred one heedless day,
>This heart take Thou to scan
>   Both within and without:
>Refine with fire it gold,
>   Purge Thou its dross away--
>Yea hold it in Thy hold,
>   Whence none can pluck it out.
>
>I take my heart in my hand--
>   I shall not die, but live--
>Before Thy face I stand;
>   I, for Thou callest such:
>All that I have I bring,
>   All that I am I give,
>Smile Thou and I shall sing,
>   But shall not question much. (Crump 1, 125)

"Although Rossetti considers the married and the unmarried life to be in 'gracious harmony,' she sees the life of the married woman, especially her spiritual life, as much less satisfying than that of the unmarried woman, for the wife must approach God indirectly through her husband," as D'Amico discusses ("Eve, Mary, and Mary Magdalene . . ." 181). A wife's duty might bring pain and difficulty; therefore, it was safer and better to remain a daughter rather than to become a wife (181). In *Letter and Spirit* (1883) and in *Face of the Deep* (1892), as William Rossetti explains (lxxi), Rossetti makes it clear that in Genesis after the fall, Adam sins when he tries to shelter himself from God's wrath at the expense of Eve. Because of this, it is better for women to trust in God and not in men. Rossetti's concern about the relationship of woman to the world and to God is reflected in the poem "Twice" in the use of "O my love' and "O my God" and in the frequent use of "I" which relates to the "eye" as the window to the soul.

Another similar repetition is "O my soul" in "Shall I Forget?" from February of 1865 (Rossetti, William 374). Female nothingness is also related in this poem to God's promise of "nothing" -- that if, as the Tractarians believed, a Christian woman was forebearant and lived a life that paralleled Christ's suffering, she would be rewarded with the "peace of Paradise."

> Shall I forget on this side of the grave?
> I promise nothing: you must wait and see
>   Patient and brave.
> (O my soul, watch with him and he with me.)
>
> Shall I forget in peace of Paradise?
> I promise nothing: follow, friend, and see
>   Faithful and wise.
> (O my soul, lead the way he walks with me). (Crump 1, 153)

Christina Rossetti's identified with Eve's loss of innocence. Through the fall, Eve brought not only pain and death to the world but a sense of isolation for all women. The blood of Christ is related to rebirth and the blood of passion and birth in Rossetti's poem "Despised and Rejected." These concepts are also evident in the poem "If Only" and in many of her other poems from 1860 until Rossetti's death.

The Tractarian concepts of human isolation, faith in the afterlife, and nature's cycle as a testament to the immutability of heaven are apparent in the sonnet "If Only" composed in February of 1865 (Rossetti, William 244):

>If I might only love my God and die!
>>But now he bids me love Him and live on,
>>Now when the bloom of all my life is gone,
>>The pleasant half of life has quite gone by.
>My tree of hope is lopped that spread so high;
>>And I forget how Summer glowed and shone,
>>While Autumn grips me with its fingers wan,
>>And frets me with its fitful windy sigh.
>When Autumn passes then must Winter numb,
>>And Winter may not pass a weary while,
>>>But when it passes Spring shall flower again:
>And in that Spring who weepeth now shall smile,
>>Yea, they shall wax who now are on the wane,
>Yea, they shall sing for love when Christ shall come. (Crump 1, 181)

Christina Rossetti pictured herself and all Victorian women as "A Daughter of Eve," published in September 1865, as William Rossetti points out (379):

>>A fool I was to sleep at noon,
>>>And wake when night is chilly
>>Beneath the comfortless cold moon;
>>A fool to pluck my rose too soon,
>>>A fool to snap my lily.

>>My garden-plot I have not kept;
>>>Faded and all-forsaken,
>>I weep as I have never wept:
>>Oh it was summer when I slept,
>>>It's winter now I waken

>>Talk what you please of future Spring
>>>And sun-warmed sweet tomorrow:--

>Stripped bare of hope and everything,
>No more to laugh no more to sing,
>I sit alone with sorrow. (Crump 1, 208)

Rossetti pictured Eve in her poems "Eve" and in "Bird or Beast?" weeping "alone with sorrow." Tears appear in *Goblin Market* as a symbol of heaven's grace. Tears in medieval literature often are a sign of baptism or forgiveness or a manifestation of Christ's love and sacrifice for mankind, according to Nancy Harvey (173). This is paralleled in "A Daughter of Eve," in "If Only," and in Christina Rossetti's personal situation as she grows older. This is the fate of all daughters of Eve, especially the fallen ones, who were "A fool to pluck [the] rose too soon,/A fool to snap [the] lily" (ll. 4, 5, Crump 1, 208). The untended garden of Eden mentioned in "Eve" and in "Balm in Gilead" is also referred to in "Daughter of Eve." The garden of Eden is a metaphor for the fallen status of womankind that can be redeemed by involvement in creation, either artistic or procreative. Heaven's garden is also related to Christ's mother and to female sexuality in many pieces of medieval literature, as David Holbrook professes (103). Contributing to the creation/redemption cycle will bring the redeemed woman to the heavenly paradise of Christ's love.

In "Cousin Kate," written in November 1859 (Rossetti, William 347). Christina Rossetti concludes with the concepts of "wedding ring" and "coronet" (Crump 1, 31, ll. 43 and 48). These circular images are related to the female orifices and cycle as well as to the grandeur of God's eternal love and the loss of innocence which are themes Rossetti pursues in her "Eve" poetry and in *Goblin Market*. The coronet relates to Christ's regal crown as God and to the crown of thorns, the punishment of man's fallen status brought about by Eve's disobedience and redeemed by Christ's love. In the poem "Spring," written in 1859 as William Rossetti observes (346), the "seeds" and "stone of fruits" tell "of the hidden life/That breaks forth underneath,/Life nursed in its grave by Death" (Crump 1, 34, ll. 1-9). Christ is the seed of "hidden life" (l. 7) for Rossetti. God instigated the cycle of creation, life and death, perpetuated by Eve, Mary, and all women. In this same poem, Rossetti reveals that "the sun has power," (l. 27) that the cycle of the seasons/the cycle of creation is related to "the Son" of God who has power over life and death.

In "An 'Immurata' Sister," written in 1865 as William Rossetti suggests (380), Rossetti states in stanza two that "Men work and think, but women/feel"(l. 5, Crump 2, 120). In this same stanza, she indicates that "And so (for I'm a woman, I)/And so I should be glad to die" (l. 6 and 7). In stanza three of "An 'Immurata' Sister," the author reveals that

> Hearts that die, by death renew
> their youth,
>
> Lightened of this life that doubts
> and dies;
> Silent and contented, while the
> Truth
> Unveiled makes them wise. (Crump 2, 120)

These references explore the "pregnant" silence of heaven's peace, not like the silence of the Victorian woman on earth. Since it is the woman's role to feel as Eve does in Rossetti's poem "Eve," a woman will be finally free of her fallen status, of her oppressed state in the patriarchy, in heaven's silences.

Christina Rossetti "defined herself in terms of a divine relationship that was begun in God, sustained by God, and in the end would live eternally with God," as Vickie Smith asserts (31). The field of flowers with its hidden terrors in Rossetti's "Amor Mundi," published in 1865, as William Rossetti explains (375), is a good example of the Tractarian belief that Nature is a link between mankind and the divine, that the material world constantly tested one's faith in God. "'Oh what is that glides quickly where velvet flowers grow thickly,/ Their scent comes rich and sickly?'--'A scaled and hooded worm'" (ll. 13-6, Crump 1, 214). This "worm" not only represents death brought about by Eve's fall from grace but also Satan and the goblin men in *Goblin Market*.

Eve's fall was the impetus for the suppressed state of women in the Victorian world. Rossetti believed women should keep to their place in Victorian society even though she did assert her creative power when she disagreed with her brother Dante Gabriel and she did leave her brother William enough money to pay him back for his twenty years of financial support. "To seek a higher place was to do as Eve had done 'when she postponed obedience to knowledge'" (D'Amico "Eve, Mary, and Mary Magdalene..." 180). A later poem that focuses on the same theme is "Golden Silence" written before 1882 (Rossetti, William 406). However, in this poem, Rossetti now envisions the silence of Eve and the daughters of Eve as only earthbound. In heaven, the Victorian woman would finally find a voice as is apparent in the lines "But whoso reaps the ripened corn/Shall shout in his delight,/While silences vanish away" (ll. 13-5, Crump 2, 106). Eve had brought the silence of death into the world, but all women could voice their joy in Christ's love and life everlasting in heaven.

> There is silence that saith 'Ah me!'
> There is silence that nothing saith;
> One the silence of life forlorn,
> One the silence of death;
> One is, and the other shall be.
>
> One we know and have known for long,
> One we know not, but we shall know,
> All we who have ever been born;
> Even so, be it so,--
> There is silence, despite a song.
>
> Sowing day is silent day,
> Resting night is a silent night;
> But whoso reaps the ripened corn
> Shall shout in his delight,
> While silences vanish away. (Crump 2, 106)

This poem connects the suffering of life and the "silence" of death. The silences of the world are not like the silences of heaven's rewards. Another poem with a similar message is "De Profundis" written before 1882 (Rossetti, William 398). The transience of this world compared to the eternity of heaven's fulfillment of desire is expressed in the lines "But all my heart is one desire,/And all in vain:/For I am bound with fleshly bands,/Joy, beauty, lie beyond my scope;/I strain my heart, I stretch my hands,/And catch at hope" (ll. 11-6, Crump 2, 94). The imagery of the female heart connected to the hearts of Eve and Christ and of hope deferred to the afterlife are present in this and many of her poems.

In Christina Rossetti's notes for her devotional prose work on *Genesis*, she makes as association between Eve who came from Adam's side and the Church built from the side of Christ. The first sonnet in *Later Life* written before 1882 reflects *Genesis*

(Rossetti, William 82). Adam and Eve leave paradise in sonnet 14, and sonnet 15 is a flashback on the fall. The relationship between Eve, Adam, and God is explored in sonnets 14 and 15. In sonnet 15, Rossetti iterates, "Let woman fear to teach and bear to learn,/Remembering the first woman's mistake" (ll. 1 and 2, Crump 2, 144). This reflects the relationship between the Eve-like Laura and the Mary-like Lizzie in *Goblin Market*. Sonnet 28 is a mirror of the after-life where the dead are "brimful of knowledge they many not impart,/Brimful of love for you and love for me" (ll. 12-4, Crump 2, 150). These lines are juxtaposed to scripture concerning the evil knowledge obtained by consuming the fruit from the forbidden tree versus eating the fruit of Christ's love in repentance. The dead live in the Eden that humanity lost in its fallen state.

In *Letter and Spirit*, published in 1883 as William Rossetti explains (lxxi), Christina Rossetti states:

> She sees not face to face, but as it were in a glass darkly. Every thing, and more than all every person, and most of all the one best beloved person, becomes her mirror wherein she beholds Christ and her shrine wherein she serves Him [but] she whose heart is virginal [. . .] beholds the King in His beauty; wherefore she forgets by comparison her own people and her father's house. Her Maker is her Husband, endowing her with a name better than of sons and of daughters. (Rossetti, Christina *Letter and Spirit: Notes on the Commandments* 91-92)

The unmarried woman gives all to God. "She contemplates Him and abhors herself in dust and ashes. She contemplates Him, and forgets herself in Him" (92). She is nothingness made strong in God. Christina Rossetti always envisioned Eve's fall as directly parallel with her own redemption, as D'Amico illustrates ("Eve, Mary, and Mary Magdalene . . ." 191). Genesis may have told of Eve's shame but Revelations told of woman's glory. Milton's *Paradise Lost* speaks of Eve's guilt, but *Paradise Regained* does not reveal the glory of woman. Ultimately, Rossetti reveals in *Face of the Deep* that "she [Eve and all her daughters] will be made equal with men and angels" (312).

Rossetti's prose work *Time Flies* from 1885 according to William Rossetti (lxxi) describes the sentiment of the healing power of Christ's love for the repentant sinner, in this case, Mary Magdalene who was another redeemed, fallen woman:

> A record of this Saint is a record of love. She ministered to the Lord of her substance, she stood by the Cross, she sat over against the Sepulchre, she sought Christ in the empty grave, and

> found Him and was found of Him in the contiguous garden. Yet this is that same Mary Magdalene out of whom aforetime He had cast seven devils. Nevertheless, the golden cord of love we are contemplating did all along continue unbroken in its chief strand: for before she loved Him, He loved her. (Rossetti, Christina *Time Flies* 139-40)

The last paragraph of this passage reiterates the importance of the circle that was created by Eve's original fall that connects herself through God to the creation of Christ. Christ in turn redeemed the sins of all fallen souls. As part of the Godhead, however, he also created Eve. Eve's naiveté is also stressed in *Time Flies* where Satan, the master of "guile" "cajoles" Eve's innocent nature.

In *The Face of the Deep, a Devotional Commentary on the Apocalypse* written in 1892 according to William Rossetti (lxxi), Christina Rossetti defines the "daughters of Eve":

> We daughters of Eve may beyond her sons be kept humble by that common voice which makes temptation feminine. Woman is a mighty power for good or for evil. She constrains though she cannot compel. Potential for evil, it becomes her to beware and forbear; potential for good, to spend herself and be spent for her brethren. (Rossetti, Christina *Face of the Deep* 357-8)

The reference to forbearance here is reminiscent of the Tractarian tenets of asceticism and sisterhood symbolic in Lizzie's actions in *Goblin Market*. The power of women is related here to the fallen angels in *Genesis* who also had great potential for good or evil. Temptation and redemption are specifically the feminine weakness and strength. These attributes are directly related to the life of Christ, a life of temptation, humility, asceticism, goodness, and redemption.

> Eve exhibits one extreme of feminine character [. . .] Eve parleyed with a devil [. . .] Eve sought knowledge [. . .] Eve aimed at self-indulgence [. . .] Eve, by disbelief and disobedience, brought sin to the birth [. . .] And yet [. . .] so (I humbly hope and trust) amongst all saints of all time will stand before the Throne, Eve the beloved first Mother of us all. Who that has loved and revered her own immediate dear mother, will not echo the hope? (Rossetti, Christina *Face of the Deep* 310-1)

To Christina Rossetti, Eve, like herself, was "the disobedient daughter who broke God's law (D'Amico "Eve, Mary, and Mary Magdalene . . ." 175). However, Eve and

Christina Rossetti were also creators who redeemed their sins and would hopefully one day "stand before the Throne" in heaven.

In *Face of the Deep*, Christina Rossetti also commented that "Penitence *must*, on pain of ultimate rejection, recover purity and guilelessness" (354). This is why Eve in Genesis and Laura in *Goblin Market* are saved by Christ's love; they both deeply repented their sins. All fallen women, in Victorian society and in Rossetti's poems like "Margery," "An Apple-Gathering," Cousin Kate," Songs in a Cornfield," and "From sunset to star rise," could be so redeemed, as D'Amico indicates ("Eve, Mary, and Mary Magdalene . . ." 188).

In the poem "Our Mothers" written before 1893, as William Rossetti asserts (214), Christina Rossetti outlines the pain of female nothingness in the world and the joy women find in sisterhood and in paradise. These women tell the living in the poem to "'Learn as we learned in life's/sufficient school, Work as we worked in patience of/our rule,/Walk as we walked, much less/by sight than faith,/Hope as we hoped, despite our/slips and scathe,/Fearful in joy and confident in dule'" (ll.6-15, Crump 2, 292). This is the fate of Eve's daughters after the fall, redeemed after death in the joy of Heaven's Eden: "How looking back to earth/from Paradise/Do tears not gather in those/loving eyes?--/Ah happy eyes!" (ll. 11-3, Crump 2, 292). The eyes, which are vacant with the sin of the fall, become "loving" and "happy" when filled with God's redemption.

Rossetti's poem "Go in Peace," written before 1893, as William Rossetti observes (136), reassures the reader of the miracles God's love can do including the cleansing of the fallen status of woman:

> Can peach renew lost bloom,
> Or violet lost perfume,
> Or sullied snow turn white as overnight?
> Man cannot compass it, yet never fear:
> The leper Naaman
> Shows what God will and can;
> God Who worked there is working here;
> Wherefore let shame, not gloom, betinge thy brow,
> God Who worked then is working now. (Crump 2 321)

The Creation/Redemption Cycle

Critic Augustine Birrell in Victorian times stated that "Eve is, I think, more interesting than 'Heaven-born Helen, Sparta's queen,'--I mean in herself, and as a woman to write poetry about" (qtd in Nelson 11). Christina Rossetti agreed with this statement. According to Mary Sullivan, Eve had been one of the primary role models for women for thousands of years (16). *Seek and Find*, Christina Rossetti's prose work published in 1879 by the Society for Promoting Christian Knowledge (SPCK), is divided into two sections: "The First Series: Creation" and "The Second Series: Redemption," as Scheinberg points out (246). Clearly, near the end of Rossetti's life, she was assimilating all her poetic experience about Eve and Eve's part in the origination of creation and redemption in women's religious lives.

"Creation" and "Redemption" are the two most important aspects of woman's relationship to God. God had created woman, woman had been tempted and fell, woman had created the Redeemer, and Christ had restored grace to mankind. Rossetti accepts this aspect of a woman's place in God's kingdom without vanity. In "Ice and Snow," part of "Redemption," Rossetti says, "Let us imitate the practical examples of [the] virtuous woman...and copying her we shall become trustworthy, loving, prudent, diligent...it will do us no harm to recognize...a figure of the Church: that great Mother and Mistress...who because her whole family was washed and beautified in the blood of Christ...has no need to fear" (ll. 223-4, Scheinberg 250). Eve, Mary, and the Church are the "great Mother and Mistress." Rossetti sees woman's position in the patriarchy, social and religious, as a parallel to Christ's. Non-assertiveness and the ability to minister were parts of Victorian female identity and part of Christ's character. Women must learn to obey as Christ was subordinate to God. Women are therefore "the true imitators of Christ" on earth.

Rossetti's poetry is full of allusions to woman's proper role and to the evils of female ego. In Sonnet 14 of *Later Life* written before 1882, Rossetti states "She [Eve] propped upon his strength, and he in guise/Of lover tho' of lord, girt to fulfil/Their term of life and die when God should will" (ll. 5-7, Crump 2, 144). The married woman, like Eve, should be sustained by her husband's "strength" as he is lord in her life. The Tractarians, however, put importance on the celibate life; therefore, religion was the sustaining "strength" in Rossetti's life. Women in Victorian society were considered morally superior to men and were responsible for building the foundation of a moral society, according to Scheinberg (21). This is reflected in the ending of *Goblin Market* where Laura and Lizzie are at peace in their domestic surroundings with Laura preaching to the children the moral axiom: "For there is no friend like a sister" (l. 562, Crump 1, 26). Lizzie's role in this poem is to save her sister from evil temptation. The superior role of woman as moral teacher in Victorian society is an integral part of female existence, paralleling for the Tractarians the role of Christ as moral instructor. "Religious affiliation is always an inherent part of the poet's construction of self as part of...a larger 'English' community" (Scheinberg 38).

However, Rossetti also warns women in *Later Life*, Sonnet 15 of the evil of ego in assuming the role of moral teacher. "Let women fear to teach and bear to learn,/Remembering the first woman's first mistake./Eve has for pupil the inquiring snake,/Whose doubts she answered on a great concern;/But he the tables so contrived to turn" (ll. 1-5, Crump 2, 144). Tractarian humility is emphasized in this poem. Victorian female poets were attempting to create a voice, to define an identity in the literary world. Rossetti saw the Victorian female religious identity as inseparable from the vision of the mother icon, Eve, as a part of the creation/redemption cycle.

Christina Rossetti explains the significance of the fall in terms of gender by stating in the prose work *Letter and Spirit* that

> It is in no degree at variance with the Sacred Record to picture to ourselves Eve, that first and typical woman, [with]...a castle-building spirit...a feminine boldness and directness of aim...Her very virtues may have opened the door to temptation. By birthright gracious and accessible, she lends an ear to all petitions...she never suspects even the serpent. Eve preferred various prospects of God's Will: Adam seems to have preferred one person to God: Eve diverted her "mind" and Adam his "heart' from God Almighty. Both courses led to one common result, that is, to one common ruin (Gen.3). Whatever else may be deduced from the opening chapters of *Genesis*, their injunction of obedience is plainly written; of unqualified obedience, of obedience on pain of death. (Rossetti, Christina *Letter and Spirit: Notes on the Commandments* 18-19)

Feminine imagination and creativity is complimented in this passage. Misuse of imagination and disobedience to God's laws cause the original sin which creates a sense of "hope deferred" until the afterlife. Rossetti uses this line from Proverbs 13.12 many times in her poetry. Guilt and hope are repeated themes in Rossetti's "Eve" poetry. The following is an excerpt from an Office-hymn for Passion Sunday which Rossetti was acquainted with and makes the connection between the tree of forbidden fruit and Christ's cross:

> When [man] fell on death by tasting
> Fruit of the forbidden tree
> Then another tree was chosen
> Which the world from death should free. (Battiscombe 108)

Many of Rossetti's works have a hymn-like quality. There is a purity about Christina Rossetti's feeling of *eros* and a passion about her attitude toward *agape* in many of her poems.

Rossetti's works undercut the manmade hierarchies (patriarchal Victorian standards and mores) which hinder mankind from attaining God's grace, the hierarchies which dominate Milton's *Paradise Lost*. During the reign of Queen Victoria, women constructed two responses to their subordination in the patriarchy: they challenged it through the political movement of suffrage and attempted to "assimilate into the domestic role Christian patriarchy had constructed for [them]," as Scheinberg ponders (21). Christina Rossetti was not a suffragette. She supported the two "spheres" of life in Victorian society: the public sphere of men and the domestic sphere of women. Most of Christina Rossetti's influences were male. Rossetti does not completely nor successfully break from the male constructs concerning women in her writing. However, her poetry and the writings of other 18th and 19th-century women writers paved the way for 20th-century feminists like Elaine Showalter and Helene Cixous. Christina Rossetti was a godmother for future female writers; Rossetti's "sisterhood" lives on in the 20th century.

Adhering to Victorian conventions, Rossetti would view Eve's fall as part of her disobedience to her married place in the patriarchy. Paying homage to earthly vanities rather than the rewards of the world to come--this is the sin of Eve. Eve "experiences sin, not at the Tree of Life with Satan, but in her dream; it allows her to envision what eventually captivates her mind during the temptation," as Christopher Forget interrogates (4). "Eve's fall from grace--her radical curiosity--set in motion the wheels of salvation" (Harrison, Antony, *Christina Rossetti in Context* 56). In Rossetti's poetry, she attempts to purify this sin of humanity.

In the Bible, women as the daughters of Eve, are saved from the original sin through the bearing of children. God's prophesy of Eve as the mother of mankind delineates Eve as a redeemer of mankind before and after the Fall, in other words, that she saves, she is saved for, and she is saved by her capacity for motherhood, as Philip Gallagher discusses (27). In Christina Rossetti's poetry, Eve and her words have a healing power due to her connection to Christ. John Shawcross states that there is definitely a parallel between Eve and Jesus as redemptive images in Genesis due to their subordinated places in the hierarchy (*The Self and the World* 49). Christina Rossetti sees this redemptive connection between Eve and Jesus as part of a cycle and not as part of a hierarchal relationship. All of the daughters of Eve participate in creation to redeem the calamities, wars and debauchery of the world that Eve's sin had let loose, as Wittreich argues (15).

Milton's celebration of the creative power of woman in *Paradise Lost* as conducted in the name of the masculine is something Christina Rossetti would have found abhorrent, according to William Zunder and Suzanne Trill (57). The concept that women were commodities, tokens of exchange in a patriarchy and that therefore, authority and authorship were a solely masculine function was totally alien to Christina Rossetti's philosophy, religious beliefs, and self-concept. Christina Rossetti believed true freedom was obedience to God's laws, one of which was that creation was female and could come in the form of bearing children or creating in some other manifestation, as through writing. Concerning woman's place in the creation cycle, Karen Horney expostulates that

> first of all, woman's capacity to give birth is partly denied and partly devaluated: Eve was made from Adam's rib and a curse was put on her to bear children in sorrow. In the second place, by interpreting her tempting Adam to eat of the tree of knowledge, as a sexual temptation, woman appears as the sexual temptress, who plunges man into misery. I believe that these two elements, one born out of resentment, the other out of anxiety, have damaged the relationship between the sexes from the earliest times to the present. (Horney 318)

Woman's capacity to love, console, and purify are the things Christina Rossetti emphasized in her poetry about relationships. "Love and childbirth, its physical offspring, are emblematic of Christ's presence" (LoTempio 121). Christina Rossetti, although not a mother herself, was very aware of "Christ's presence" in childbirth, so much so that from 1873 to 1893 she wrote a series of nursery rhyme, sing-song poems for children (Rossetti, William 426). The illegitimate child was a constant reminder in Victorian society of the woman's loss of innocence and banishment from proper married society. However, Christina Rossetti presents in her poems "A Triad," "Light Love," and "Margery" that the difference between fallen and unfallen status in women is invisible. All women have the potential to be the objects of seduction and betrayal as in her poem *Goblin Market.*

The female contribution to mankind as Eve's legacy is displayed in the poem "A Helpmeet for Him," written before 1891, as William Rossetti indicates (415). The title of this poem paraphrases a line from Genesis, that describes the relationship between Adam and Eve.

> Woman was made for man's delight:
> Charm, O woman, be not afraid!
> His shadow by day, his moon by night,
> Woman was made.
>
> Her strength with weakness is overlaid;
> Meek compliances veil her might;
> Him she stays by whom she is stayed.
>
> World-wide champion of truth and right,
> Hope in gloom and in danger aid,
> Tender and faithful, ruddy and white,
> Woman was made. (Crump 2, 169)

This poem extols the virtues of the ideal Victorian woman who by bearing the silence and lower station of a woman in this time period shows her strength of forbearance as in the lines "Meek compliances veil her might" (l. 6). This ameliorates the sin of the original fall. The Victorian woman must emulate the original mother Eve who was "hope in gloom and in danger aid" (l. 9) to Adam. The line "Him she stays by whom she is stayed" (l. 7) not only refers to a woman's husband and the fidelity between them but also to the Tractarian connection of love between postulant and Christ.

As Mayberry illustrates, "Finally, for Rossetti, the miracle of poetic creation is its potential for discovery, its ability to reveal the powerfully reforming truth" (54). "The power of the female symbol found in Christian ideology enabled Rossetti to carry out a radical transformation that would empower [herself]," as Melanie Plowman suggests (1). This "female symbol" is embodied in the person of Eve for Christina Rossetti. "The Thread of Life," written before 1882, as William Rossetti explains (263), examines Rossetti's reconciliation with her status as a daughter of Eve. "Thus am I mine own prison. Everything/ Around me free and sunny and at ease . . . I am not what I have nor what I do;/But what I was I am, I am even I" (ll. 15-6 and 27-8, Crump 2, 123). Nowhere is the assertion that "poetic creation" expressed Rossetti's self-empowerment more poignantly argued than in "The Iniquity of the Fathers Upon the Children." The lines that follow are the final lines of the poem and sum up Christina Rossetti's view of herself as a daughter of Eve, as a bride of Christ, and as a child of God.

Christina Rossetti used her poems and prose from 1860 to the end of her life to assist her in a personal quest to fuse the entities of Laura and Lizzie from *Goblin Market,* the fallen woman and the redeemer, inside Rossetti's own soul. At the end of her life, Christina Rossetti made peace with the pain of being a daughter of Eve and accepted the hardship of waiting for the justice, peace, and the power of voice awaiting in the afterlife:

> I'll not blot out my shame
> With any man's good name;
> But nameless as I stand,
> My hand is my own hand,
> And nameless as I came
> I go to the dark land.
>
> 'All equal in the grave'--
> I bide my time till then:
> 'All equal before God'--
> Today I feel His rod,
> Tomorrow He may save:
>   Amen. (Crump 1, 178)

The world of reserve of the Oxford Movement and the world of sensuality of the Pre-Raphaelites were in opposition, and Christina Rossetti began to reconcile these differences in her early poetry concerning Eve. Eve, like Christina Rossetti, had been torn between the sensuality of the material world and obedience to God's laws and will. Christina Rossetti saw that this conflict was resolved through the fall and redemption of mankind. Women as creators/procreators were an essential part of mankind's birth and death which reconciles the Pre-Raphaelite mutable world with the Tractarian immutable world to come, which fills the void of female nothingness left by the original sin. The vanity of the material world existed due to the fall of Eve. The fallen world was corrupted, not like Eden, which was free of lust. Even so, God's presence could still be discovered in Nature (Lo Tempio 103). Nature was a link between fallen man and the divine. The greatest test of faith was the material world, for Christina Rossetti and for Eve (115). *Goblin Market* is a crucial poem in Rossetti's development of her version of Eve, which contains the elements of the natural world's vanity and temptation which creates a vacuum, an emptiness in a woman's soul that only God can fill.

    A different type of "dark land" for Rossetti was her envisionment of the consumed consumer; Chapter 3 uses Marxist literary theory to examine Rossetti's epic poem *Goblin Market*.

CHAPTER 3
What We Owe: Bankruptcy in *Goblin Market*

English poet Christina Rossetti scrutinizes the fear of bankruptcy in her parable of power relations *Goblin Market,* published in 1862. The merchant men in Rossetti's "A Peep at The Goblins" (the original title of the poem *Goblin Market;* the full text of the poem is in Appendix I) reveal the world of the salesman in Victorian England. Rossetti's poem gives the reader a "peek" at the world of English consumerism.

Economics in Victorian England

The mid to later 19th century in England was an era of retail revolution, as Margot Finn discusses (278). General limited liability was a common practice with businessmen in nineteenth-century England; the insurgence of limited liability created new opportunities to defraud creditors (Foreman-Peck 5). "Let the buyer beware" were never truer words. In English Victorian business, there were few restraints on how money could be made. Financial irregularities abounded in personal and commercial bookkeeping. Company promoters, like Ernest Terah Hooley, were renowned for their ability to exaggerate the true value of their company's worth in stock exchange; this is how Hooley obtained his commissions (Foreman-Peck 7). Buyers were deceived into buying "watered" company stocks. "Competition was calculated to ensure the survival of the most unscrupulous supplier" (7). Public attitudes became critical of immoral business practices.

Eric Hobsbawm, a political and social historian, indicates that personal insolvency was extremely serious, because there was no form of social security or government assistance in Victorian England as exists in contemporary times:

> A man might have to work hard to raise himself into the middle class, but once in a moderately flourishing line of business, he could take things very easily indeed, unless he made some appalling miscalculation, or hit an abnormally bad patch in the course of an abnormally bad slump. Bankruptcy was, according to economic theory, the penalty of inefficient businessmen, and its spectre haunts the novels of Victorian

England [. . .] the very horror of bankruptcy is itself a symptom of its comparative rarity. (Hobsbawm 161-2)

V. Markham Lester concurs that the validity of financial disaster was a significant issue for English Victorian society; random factors often ruined a family. Although insolvency declined near the end of the century after the Great Depression between 1873 and 1896, financial failure was indeed a real threat (Lester 171). Rossetti wrote *Goblin Market* a decade before the Great Depression when the Bankruptcy Lists of *The Gazette* were an ever-present testament to the decay of life underlying the surface prosperity of the era, as Weiss discusses (14).

In 1843, *Punch Magazine* published Thomas Hood's poem, *The Song of the Shirt*. This powerful indictment of capitalism was supported by cartoons such as *Capital and Labour* and *Cheap Clothing*, by John Leech, that illustrated the growth of inequality that was taking place in Britain during the 1840s. The magazine also campaigned against the Corn Laws, the 1834 Poor Law and reform of parliament ("Punch Magazine" 1). Years later during the Great Depression, E. H. Shepard's "Gobbling Market," a satiric cartoon based on Rossetti's poem, appeared in *Punch* magazine. In the cartoon, a snail is selling the shell off his back, a chicken is selling its own eggs with dead chickens roasting in the background, and a parrot is making a sale to a customer. Almost all of the salesmen and customers in the cartoon have claws for hands. The rat salesman is dressed in a fancy waistcoat with a watch fob. The cat is selling ladies' stockings with a sign that reads "No Coupons." A sign posted on a tree says "This way to the fines pool." Shepard's depiction of the goblin men from Rossetti's poem shows the seamy side of the sales profession in any era. In the world of *Goblin Market*, all roads lead to the "fines pool."

Marxist Critical Theory and *Goblin Market*

Creating and experiencing literary works is about producing and consuming. *Goblin Market* ends with Laura "producing" stories for her children's consumption, as an author of her own life. The children consume stories rather than the poisoning wares of the "merchant men." Laura's life at the end of the poem is a life of production, of children and stories, separate from the hazards of dealing with the goblin men in their marketplace. Living in industrialized England, Christina Rossetti was a patroness of the arts expressed in her poetry and prose. Her poem *Goblin Market* is a reaction to the commodification of culture and the arts of which the

Victorians were becoming cognizant (Gagnier 43). The arts were being "bankrupt" by commodification.

Like Elizabeth Barrett Browning's heroine in *Aurora Leigh*, Rossetti's "Laura," at the end of the poem, is a mother and an author, a creator/producer in different capacities set in opposition to industrial capitalism. Christina Rossetti was aware of the fact that women were undervalued in Victorian society as producers and consumers (49). Rossetti would have agreed with Sylvia Walby's statement that "within the patriarchal mode of production the producing class is composed of housewives or domestic labourers, while the non-producing and exploiting class is composed of husbands" (52). In *Goblin Market*, Laura and Lizzie's husbands are non-existent and the goblin men exploit the women. Rossetti had personal knowledge of working class women who bore illegitimate children and their hardships by working at a home for fallen women managed by All Saints Sisterhood as part of her Tractarian faith. These women were bankrupt: economically, spiritually, socially. Christina Rossetti was opposed to the victimization of women by the patriarchy; just as Laura is a slave to the powers of the goblin men, the women who were assisted by the sisterhood had been consumed by the economy of English Victorian society.

People feel alienated because they are objectified; they feel like they have become commodities in the labor system, as Leonard Jackson argues (66). Laura in *Goblin Market* is a commodity; she sells part of her body, a lock of hair, to buy the fruit (l. 126). She is used and thrown away by the goblin men when she is of no more use to them. Laura feels alienated from her former life. Rossetti shows the interplay and outcome when the marketplace takes precedent over agrarian life. During Victorian times, there was a developing hedonism, the privileging of consumption, standing in opposition to the old philosophy of asceticism associated to the work ethic (Gagnier 52). Laura represents this out of control consumption and desire for pleasure at all costs, and Lizzie represents the old order of stoicism.

"The language of Christina Rossetti's best-known poem, *Goblin Market*, is remarkably mercantile" (Helsinger 189). Thus begins Elizabeth K. Helsinger's article where she discusses Rossetti's poem not as a narrative of "temptation, fall, and redemption" (189) but as "the relation of women to those markets of the nursery tales" (189). Nursery tales are full of imagery of the marketplace. Helsinger's article traverses feminist and Marxist schools of criticism just as Rossetti's poem transgresses the boundaries of serious poetry and children's poetry, morality and economy, natural creativity and alienated labour of capitalist production, female and male, fallen woman and chaste woman. All women are "agents of consumption" (Helsinger 190) just like Laura and Lizzie in *Goblin Market*.

Rossetti was aware of the sameness between the fallen and chaste woman in society's sexual marketplace, because she compared bourgeois women to aristocratic women, the women with illegitimate children and the prostitutes who frequented the Tractarian home for unwed mothers at Highgate Penitentiary where Christina Rossetti did volunteer work in comparison to women like Elizabeth Siddal, Dante Gabriel Rossetti's (Rossetti's brother) mistress, whom he misused. The women at Highgate that Christina Rossetti worked with in 1861, one year before she wrote *Goblin Market*, had ended up at Highgate due to "some folly or misfortune that left them destitute, as Marsh indicates (*A Writer's Life* 225). From Christina Rossetti's writings, it is apparent that she "felt much compassion for the poor" (226) but had a particular abhorrence of moral bankruptcy. In the marriage marketplace, "seduced and abandoned women contemplate their married rivals as successful competitors" (Helsinger 198).

Rossetti's message is that courtship is "an economic transaction" (200) and fallen women and unmarried women are laid low by a sense of emotional bankruptcy. Female beauty, reduced to currency, has tenuous power and a perishable exchange value. Women are the objects and the agents of exchange when they use their beauty and love to bargain for economic security through marriage (201). However, there is no economy of scarcity in the marriage market (202).

In Karl Marx's 1844 manuscript "On Money," he states that money is a whore because it is passed from man to man with no real value. Money is just a means to an end. "Money is a whore is a woman" (Helsinger 207). Marx calls money a "visible God," "the alienated ability of mankind, the truly creative power" that transforms "essential powers which are really impotent… into real powers and faculties" (206). Man is constantly trying to repossess money, women, and God. The goblin men in Rossetti's poem represent these men. In *Goblin Market*, Laura uses a lock of her hair (l. 126) and one of her tears (l. 127) as currency to buy the goblin men's fruit; she prostitutes and therefore bankrupts herself morally and emotionally. However, "having placed her body in circulation, she cannot re-enter the market as consumer or as object of exchange" (Marx 209).

Although Laura still hungers for the fruit, the goblin men are not interested in her because she has become used goods in the marketplace. The goblin men search for fresh, innocent consumers who have not yet tasted of their wares. Laura is no longer a consumer; she has been consumed (209). Therefore, according to Helsinger, success for women in the marketplace depended upon prior security (Helsinger 202). Lizzie represents this kind of woman in the poem; she goes to buy the goblin men's fruit with money in her pocket. Lizzie limits the meaning of consumption to buying (210); she is not a consumer and not the consumed in the male game of desire. Lizzie buys the fruit to restore Laura's health but does not consume the fruit herself. Lizzie is not bankrupt at the end of the tale; she has remained untouched by the corrosion of consumption. Jeannie, who died from her encounter with the goblins, and Laura are consumed by desire. The strongest desire in the poem, however, is the mutual care and support between women that defeats the competitive ethos of the marketplace (Helsinger 211).

Ironically, the joys of marriage in this poem are the joys of motherhood in a fantasy world without fathers (212). In the idealistic ending of Rossetti's *Goblin Market*, the sisterhood rather than the male economic structure prevails. Women's work, untouched by the political economy of the dominant male world, was a real-world impossibility. Dante Gabriel mediated the revision and production of Christina Rossetti's writing. Her writing was sullied by patriarchal interference at home and in the marketplace (Helsinger 196). Female security depended on male society. Rossetti as a female author was conscious of her "undervalued" place in the literary marketplace (196. "Women can more easily sell themselves than what they can produce—and to its consequence: if they enter the marketplace, they risk being literally consumed" (197). Male interference bankrupts Christina Rossetti's art. Male, class, and financial supremacy are argued and displaced in Rossetti's poems.

Marx's texts suggest that women must possess the power of money and must resist male mastery of money through women to be successful consumers (Helsinger 213). Rossetti understood that successful women in Victorian society withheld desire as their tool of consumer power. A successful woman also reached the status of adulthood in the patriarchy and therefore had access to speech. Laura has access to speech within the family as she tells her story to future generations, and Christina Rossetti has access to speech through her poetry (213). Also, Rossetti remained celibate which removed her from the competitive marriage market. She saw all aspects of sisterhood as "a refuge from the double threat of an exchange economy" (Helsinger 214). Rossetti's withdrawal, her reticence to play the part of consumer or consumed, may suggest the desire to hoard rather than to give and nurture. Hoarding is power (215). Withdrawl from the marketplace, symbolized in the character Lizzie in *Goblin Market*, is the only way to avoid the destructive effects of moral, spiritual, physical, and emotional bankruptcy. However, Helsinger concludes that in a world run by men, women can never completely withdraw from the economy of production and exchange (215). Bankruptcy is always a threat for all those who traverse the marketplace, those who sell and those who buy.

Goblin Market has been read as a nursery tale, a portrait of divided self, a fantasy about sex, and a parable about sisterhood. Terence Holt sees it as a parable about power relations (51). *Goblin Market* attempts to imagine a position for women outside systems of power, but its language, which cannot escape gender, undoes the attempt. Autonomy is an illusion; the poem is an assertion concerning economic forces or networks of power. Bankruptcy cannot be avoided. Rossetti's verse celebrates endurance; the poem ends with the unending struggle for women and men trying to free themselves of economic prisons (Holt 66). *Goblin Market* is about the difficulty of achieving consumer freedom; consumers are buried within consumer ideologies and blinded to assumptions that are imprisoning.

The "utopia" for the businessman in any century is that the consumer is consumed with desire for the product or service the salesman is selling, so consumed in fact that the buyer will seek out and buy the product or service at absolutely any cost. The consumer should be consumed with envy of those who have procured the product or service already, and so consumed by the product or service after consumption that the buyer wants more and more, making the businessman richer and richer. Sir Thomas More coined the word "utopia" which means "nowhere." The capitalist utopia is a fantasy world.

The goblin men, the fruit venders in the poem, are depicted as weasel-like, animalistic entities whose intent is to suck the life out of their customers, literally, bankrupting them. The image of the vampiric businessman in *Goblin Market* has parallels with the terror of bankruptcy that appears in English Victorian novels. Bankruptcy in real life left the tormented person in this era completely vulnerable and helpless as the character Laura is left ravaged and wanting in *Goblin Market*.

Laura is financially, emotionally, and physically bankrupt by her associations with the businessmen in the poem. The goblin salesmen, however, also represent a kind of bankruptcy – the morally bankrupt who take advantage of the innocent, the struggling working man trying to make a buck, those who will leech off anyone so that they can avoid scandal and not end up unemployed and in the poorhouse (scandal was like Greek tragedy to the Victorians in England).

Elizabeth K. Helsinger, Terence Holt, Richard Menke, and more recently Victor Mendoza, among others, have written Marxist criticism about desire, exchange and consumer power in Christina Rossetti's poem *Goblin Market*. However, there is no research that this author has uncovered showing how Rossetti's "goblin men" represent a warning about the real threat of bankruptcy in the face of unscrupulous capitalism and the dangers of buying what the "sleazy" businessman is selling in Victorian England. This essay will also interrogate the consumer reaction to these businessmen and their fear of consumerism as a path to the poor house.

My treatise on bankruptcy in relation to *Goblin Market* was influenced by Barbara Weiss' book *The Hell of the English: Bankruptcy and the Victorian Novel*. Weiss indicates that the middle years of Queen Victoria's reign, when Rossetti wrote and published *Goblin Market*, was a time when the process of industrialization had advanced to a point that English society was being restructured (13). The encroachment of capitalism was paralleled to the breakdown of traditional morality. *Goblin Market* is about failure, and failure was considered by the English Victorians to be the result of inefficiency or even lack of virtue on the part of the individual (19). The great paradox of the age was that they prided themselves on mastery of the material world and then discovered that the material took revenge upon the human spirit:

> What Georg Simmel described as 'objectivism,' what Karl Marx called 'alienation,' and what Emile Durkheim termed 'anomie,' the Victorian writers portrayed metaphorically [. . .] as 'bankruptcy' – a great social and spiritual void or apocalypse lurking ominously beneath the seeming prosperity of the Victorian years and threatening

to engulf society with it dislocations and contradictions. (qtd in Weiss 22)

This is of central importance in Rossetti's *Goblin Market*.

Bankruptcy in *Goblin Market*

William Michael Rossetti, Christina Rossetti's younger brother, warned against a search for detailed symbolism in *Goblin Market*, although he did admit to a general ethical significance for the poem:

> I have more than once heard Christina aver that the poem has not any profound or ulterior meaning--it is just a fairy story; yet one can discern that it implies at any rate this much--that to succumb to temptation makes one a victim to that same continuous temptation; that the remedy does not always lie with oneself; and that a stronger and more righteous will may prove of avail to restore one's lost estate. (Bell 207)

It is interesting that William Rossetti's interpretation of his sister's poem uses words like "to succumb to temptation makes one a victim to that same continuous temptation" and "to restore one's lost estate" (207), the very terms that would apply to a state of bankruptcy. Although Christina Rossetti demurred that her poem was "just a fairy story," Helsinger points out the number of fairy tales that focus on buying and selling (189).

The "cry" of the goblin men to "Come buy" at the opening of *Goblin Market* sounds just like the call of vendors in any town square in Victorian England, as on Charlotte Street in Christina Rossetti's childhood, as Marsh describes (*A Writer's Life* 231). One of the earliest books Christina Rossetti read was William Hone's *Everyday Book* in which a London barrow woman is crying her wares (231). The poem in the book simulates the call of the street pedlars that sounds very much like the opening lines of *Goblin Market*:

> Round and sound,
> Two-pence a pound
> Cherries! Rare ripe cherries! [. . .]
> Cherries a ha-penny a stick!
> Come and pick! Come and pick!~
> Who comes? Who comes! (Marsh 232)

This call to "buy and buy" more products would underscore for any household the magnitude of credit and debt, personal and national. According to Jon Lash, the ominous specters of credit and debt in Victorian England evoked feelings of delight and doom in their "victims of vanity" (1). 80% of sales in small city shops in England were offered on credit (1). Unpaid bills were a perpetual issue. The echoing "cry" from vendors would be a daily reminder of fiscal household issues, especially unnerving for those who were financially unsteady. Rossetti would certainly have known Covent Garden Market in London and heard the cries of Mayhew's costermongers (Menke 124). The litany of fruits that the goblin men enumerate and try to sell is reminiscent of the trade cards and billheads used by the merchants in Victorian England. Billheads were used to provide "memories of shopping experiences and communicate the marketing position of the shop as well as its topographical location; [. . . business people] used trade cards to create a consumer desire for their products that went beyond the utility value of the goods on display" (Kay 156). Trade cards included great differences of content and style with detailed descriptions of the proprietor's respectability and the quality and variety of the stock. Sometimes the trade card information was in poetic form, especially for goods and services sold to women:

> Ladies
> If you wish to buy
> Cheaper than ever, go and try,
> Babb's (High Holborn)
> That's the place,
> To suit your Purse, and Charm your Face.
> The Largest Stock in London's there,
> The Newest Patterns, rich and rare,
> Bonnets.
> Tuscans, Dunstables, Silks and Straws.
> Caps.
> Lace, Tulle, Blond, Applique, and Gauze;
> Habit shirts, Collars, Canzoves, Capes
> Of every kind, and various shapes,
> In English style, all British made
> As patronized by

85

Queen Adelaide.
An endless choice will there be found.
One shilling each, and some One Pound.
Then thither hasten, in a trice,
For now they sell at Wholesale Price.
Now ladies! now -- your attention fix.
For Babb's 296,
High Holborn. (Kay 157)

Notice the similarity of this trade card to these opening lines in Rossetti's *Goblin Market*:

"Come buy our orchard fruits,
Come buy, come buy:
Apples and quinces,
Lemons and oranges,
Plump unpecked cherries,
Melons and raspberries,
Bloom-down-cheeked peaches,
Swart-headed mulberries,
Wild free-born cranberries,
Crab-apples, dewberries,
Pine-apples, blackberries,
Apricots, strawberries;--
All ripe together
In summer weather,--
Morns that pass by,
Fair eves that fly;
Come buy, come buy:
Our grapes fresh from the vine,
Pomegranates full and fine,
Dates and sharp bullaces,
Rare pears and greengages,
Damsons and bilberries,
Taste them and try:
Currants and gooseberries,

>Bright-fire-like barberries,
>Figs to fill your mouth,
>Citrons from the South,
>Sweet to tongue and sound to eye;
>Come buy, come buy." (Rossetti, Christine, *Goblin Market*
>ll. 3-31)

This passage is the trade card of the goblin merchants, hawking their wares. Their trade card, a poetic song, tells of the obscure topographical location where the products were harvested and attempts, quite irresistibly, to create consumer desire for the product in question as well as establish a sense of propriety about the merchants themselves. Christoph Lindner indicates that early Victorian advertisers not only recognized the commodity as an object full of signification, but also used that understanding to position themselves at the place where commerce meets culture, becoming capitalism's minstrels (44). The purpose of the profusion of fruit listed on the trade card is to "overload the senses and [. . .] impair the observer's ability to see beyond the physical," as Arseneau observes ("Incarnation and Interpretation . . ." 84).

The description of the fruit on the merchant men's "trade card" is "one of the most lusciously rendered descriptions of fruit in Western literature," as Matt Christensen points out (1). "The language of the goblins' litany of enchanted fruit is sensual and indulgent" (1). In juxtaposition, the threat of figurative and literal death, since bankruptcy is a kind of death, is the undercurrent of meaning connected to the description of the fruit. The merchant men's call of "Come buy, come buy" (l. 4) is only heard by "maids" (l. 2). The matriarchal society that Rossetti creates, devoid of men except the merchants, reveals her gendering of the world of sellers and buyers. The sales world is masculine and the consumers are feminine. I do not think that Rossetti is literal here. I believe she uses masculinity to represent capitalism because she sees capitalism and industrialization as a cannibalistic, invading force and she sees consumers as innocent victims who are brutalized by the lure, the addiction of buying and buying to the point of ruin, but at the same time culpable for their addiction.

Laura is tempted by the call of the fruit sellers, but her sister, Lizzie, blushes (l. 35) at the goblins'cry. Laura's character represents the real threat of bankruptcy through intemperance, and Lizzie' character is the shame felt by insolvent families in Victorian England. Laura "bows her head" (l. 34) as she listens; this could be interpreted as a kind of misplaced reverence and surrender to the force of capitalism. However, I believe these lines indicate Lizzie's attempts to "veil" (l. 35) her embarrassment as families in Victorian England would do; the scandal would be excruciating if others found out about the debts a family, or one member of the family, had accrued.

William Thackeray presented this common fear among the middle-classes in his illustration called "An Elephant for Sale" for his novel *Vanity Fair*. He depicts a family whose belongings are suddenly taken away from them and sold at auction. The illustration enforces the essential vulgarity of the situation and the terror and humiliation that families feel who find themselves in this position: auctioneers with no knowledge of the family or the sentimental meaning of its possessions expose them to a heartless public. Dobbin, who has chivalrously come to the auction to buy back some of the Sedleys' things, appears as the helpless young gentleman threatened by the auctioneer and his two helpers, one of whom looms over the gentleman. Bankruptcy auctions were commonplace in novels of this era, as Nunokawa indicates (5). In the English Victorian novels, the bankrupt become "untouchables," helpless castaways of society, even after the debtor prisons were closed in England ("Bankruptcy in Victorian England . . ." 1).

Rossetti's Laura and Lizzie live in a pastoral environment in the poem; they work on the farm for their produce. These characters are set in opposition to the goblin men who are traveling salesmen. As Menke illustrates, the fruits of Laura and Lizzie's labor are contrasted with the fruits of the goblin men that are sold for financial gain (106). Goblins in English folklore were nomadic, just like traveling salesmen. They did not sell their wares from shops in the city. Capitalism has invaded the countryside in *Goblin Market*, a clear statement by Rossetti of the onerous nature of consumerism, an omen of the infiltration of the social structure of England by capitalism and an undermining of the agrarian economic culture of gifting, a limiting of the "cash nexus." When Laura tries to buy some of the goblin fruit in Christina Rossetti's poem, she "Long'd but had no money" (106), so she barters a lock of hair and a tear for the goods.

If middle class workers in Victorian England lost their livelihood, they had to depend on their savings, their trade union, their credit with local shopkeepers, their neighbors and friends, and the pawnbroker or the Poor Law to bail them out of financial ruin. Therefore, depicting Rossetti's main narrative figures, Lizzie and Laura, as pastoral figures makes sense. It hearkens back to an earlier time in

England's history of agrarian predominance in economic stability versus later industrialization; it reminds the reader of the power of the pastoral ethic in literature (revisiting a place of safety and security in fiction as in William Shakespeare's *As You Like It*), and it reminds the reader of Jane Austen's love of the country gentry life and skepticism of the trend to migrate to the cities to live and work (her villains, as in *Mansfield Park*, are always those who live in the city). The following lines from *Goblin Market* reveal the simplicity of country life, untarnished by industrialization:

> Early in the morning
> When the first cock crowed his warning
> Neat like bees, as sweet and busy,
> Laura rose with Lizzie:
> Fetched in honey, milked the cows,
> Aired and set to rights the house,
> Kneaded cakes of whitest wheat,
> Cakes for dainty mouths to eat,
> Next churned butter, whipped up cream,
> Fed their poultry, sat and sew'd. (ll. 199-208)

However, the characters in this idyll cannot escape the encroachment of the merchants who crawl across the glen to torment them in Rossetti's poem. No one in Victorian England could escape capitalism. In addition, the reality of country life was not always idyllic; country life required hard work with a "no pain, no gain" philosophy. The sleazy businessman represented a kind of underhanded commerce, not the honest day's work kind of labor.

Rossetti, like the other authors of this era, is commenting in *Goblin Market* on the death of a previous agrarian lifestyle in England and the skepticism of the world they have created in its place. And Rossetti knew of this nightmare first hand. Her uncle and her mother's brother, Dr John Poldori, had killed himself with poison, owing to his massive debts, according to Jan Marsh (*A Writer's Life* 15). Rossetti and her mother opened a day school at No. 38 Arlington Street, Mornington Crescent to support the family after Rossetti's father became ill and was forced to retire in 1853 (Cary 230). However, the school was not prosperous so they opened another day school in another part of town, but this school also failed. William Michael Rossetti, Christina's younger brother, writes in his memoir of his sister that their father, Gabriele Rossetti, made his living as a teacher of Italian at King's College (xlvi). However, this position paid no salary; the professors lived on a proportion of the students' fees that they were allocated, and there were never many students who wanted to learn Italian, as Marsh observes (*A Writer's Life* 21). It was family of "narrow means" since the elder Rossetti made less than 300 pounds a year, as Christina Rossetti's brother, William, discusses (xlvi). Gabriele was also an impulsive spender although his wife tried to be careful with money (Marsh *A Writer's Life* 21).

"The fortunes of the Rossetti family, always mediocre enough, were at a low ebb from 1842 to 1854, right before Christina Rossetti wrote and published *Goblin Market*. In 1843, the family worried about their financial situation and their economic state was acute (Marsh *A Writer's Life* 39). "Ill-health and partial blindness overtook our father, leading to the diminution, and ultimately, the loss, of professional employment" (Rossetti, William li). The financial burden then fell on the other members of the household: Maria, Christina's sister, became a governess. Dante, the elder brother, brought in very little due to his career in writing and painting, and his expenses were considerable. Michael Rossetti became a clerk at the Inland Revenue office (Rossetti, William li). *Goblin Market* was published in 1862, about a decade after this time of meager means. From 1854 to 1862, Christina Rossetti tried to publish her writing when her brother William took over the financial burden of keeping the family together. During this time period, Christina Rossetti made no more than a tiny 10 pounds a year as a writer (li).

The threat of bankruptcy was something that was ever-present in the family's minds. Therefore, Christina Rossetti was an expert on running from the specter of financial ruin when she wrote her poetic masterpiece. And she was not alone. *Goblin Market* is not the only work of literature written in 19th-century England that discusses financial ruin. The literature written in this era reflects a fiscal fascination; these writings (and there are many more examples than the ones listed here) depicted the idea that "sleaze" flourished in fraudulent business practices and debt was omnipresent: William Makepeace Thackeray's *Vanity Fair* (1847) and *The Newcomes* (1855); Charles Dickens's *Dombey and Son* (1848), *Bleak House* (1852), and *Little Dorrit* (1857); Charlotte Bronte's *Shirley* (1849); William Elizabeth Gaskell's *North and South* (1855), George Eliot's *The Mill and the Floss* (1860), *Silas Marner* (1861), and *Daniel Deronda* (1876); Charles Reade's *Hard Cash* (1863); and Anthony Trollopes' *The Eustace Diamonds* (1873) and *The Way We Live*

Now (1875). Insolvency touched the characters in the literature and the authors who created the characters.

William Makepeace Thackeray, Anthony Trollope, Alfred Lord Tennyson, and Thomas Babington Macaulay were all writers in 19th-century England, like Rossetti, whose families had faced bankruptcy or enormous debt. Sir Walter Scott's tragic decline was an ominous symbol of not just an author's life of financial instability, great highs and great lows, but more importantly, of a nation in crisis, as Weiss observes (16). However, the central precept of English Victorian novels was not the financial bankruptcy but things that were the same as economic ruin, bankruptcy as a metaphor.

Laura and Lizzie live in a pastoral environment, far removed from the capitalism and industrialization of city commerce. Rossetti's setting, removing her main figures from the influence of the city, is purposeful. Capitalism follows them to the country in the form of the goblin men and infiltrates their idyllic world. Capitalism is insidious, a virulent disease that penetrates all aspects of society; no one can escape it except those like Lizzie who tune out the voice of the salesman, who avoid the sales pitch, who refuse to consume. The goblin men sell fruit; this appears to be a conscious choice by Rossetti, because fruit is tempting (it hearkens back to the first temptation in the garden of Eden), and fruit is literally consumed by the consumer. Capitalism tempts the sales person to race after riches that he/she may not every achieve and tempts the consumer to buy what he/she does not really need to survive.

Although Laura appears to be protecting her sister from the strange men and their constant sales pitch, Laura is actually intrigued by their sales tactics. Laura half-heartedly tells Lizzie, all the while peaking at them:

> We must not look at goblin men,
> We must not buy their fruits:
> Who knows upon what soil they fed
> Their hungry thirsty roots? (ll. 42-45)

The thirst to consume has consumed Laura. There is also a possessiveness between Laura and the goblin men; she does not want her sister to beat her to the best buys, the good deals, so she discourages her from wanting to buy, saving the best stuff for herself. Laura discourages Lizzie by telling her that the products the merchant men are hawking must be contaminated, not the kind of produce that her "choosy" sister would want to consume. Later in the poem, Laura is unable to hear the goblin men's song after her first purchase, but Lizzie can still hear them (l. 254). Those who have "bankrupted" themselves in the "Goblin Market" are no long potential customers. "Laura turn'd cold as stone" (l. 253) with raging jealousy that her sister could consume but refuses, and Laura who desperately wants to buy more and more cannot hear the sales pitch any longer. Rossetti portrays Laura's fixation, her shop 'til you literally drop philosophy, as a type of addiction that ruins all it touches.

> Crouching close together
> In the cooling weather
> With clasping arms and cautioning lips
> With tingling cheeks and finger tips. (ll. 36-39)

The cool weather indicates that it is autumn, an image of decay. Buying and buying is decadent and can lead to financial destruction. Lines 38 and 39 are juxtaposed; being tempted to consume to the point of devastation is both frightening and thrilling. An addiction is frightening and thrilling too. In 1860, Rossetti had recurrent nightmares in which goblins, ghosts, satanic and creepy animals appeared; her tormentors were always monstrous, masculine, inescapable, and incomprehensible figures where terror and desire were mixed, as Marsh indicates ("Christina Rossetti's Vocation . . ." 257). The pairing of Laura's desire and Lizzie's shame and guilt, that March discusses as threatening erotic feelings due to the abuse of Rossetti's father towards his daughter (Marsh "Christina Rossetti's Vocation . . ." 261), I believe really indicates a parallel to the shopaholic's addictive nightmare and the threat and accompanying frustration and shame of insolvency. A number of celebrities in contemporary society have been punished for shoplifting, an addiction that is frightening and thrilling, an addiction to power and a game of chance that could end in financial disaster.

Goblins are traditionally in fairy mythology full-size devils, as Marsh discusses ("Christina Rossetti's Vocation . . ." 231). In the forties and fifties in Victorian England, Thomas Carlyle lambasted the influx of capitalism, stating that the English people had become possessed by the devil, a devil that reduced all relationships between people to a "cash nexus." The soul in this kind of world most dreaded the failure to possess money, as Weiss indicates (14). Selling is as evil business in this poem. Christina Rossetti's uncle wrote a Gothic tale called *The Vampyre* which she did not read but she possibly read Lord Byron's poem *Giaour* concerning the curse of the vampire that "ghastly haunts the native place /

And sucks the blood of thy race" as Marsh discusses (*A Writer's Life* 263). The goblin men "drain the stream of life" (263) out of their victims, just as a vampire does. The goblin men hobble (l. 47) and crawl (l. 74); they do not walk with an easy gait.

The goblins actually march up the glen backwards (l. 87) indicating the upside-down, not "upright," world of the trader. Jeff Kunowaka asserts that in the English Victorian frame of mind, "the commodity form, like a triumphal army or a thief in the night, has entranced regions of the psyche, precincts of culture and forms of labor whose worth had been measured by their distance from market value" (4). The merchants invade the psyche of the consumer. Everything becomes commodified.

Christoph Lindner explains that in *Das Capital*, Marx illustrates how capitalism and it modes of production will change the worker into a crippled monster (58). The goblins are crippled by the figurative as well as literal weight of their task: "One lugs a golden dish / Of many pounds weight" (ll. 58-59). The seller's fear of debt pushes the sales person to take advantage of the unsuspecting. The sellers have the faces of animals: cats, rats, and wombats, and ratels (ll 71, 73, 75, 76). These animals display the characteristics of sneakiness, sleaziness, and gross sensuality. Adam Smith in *An Inquiry into the Nature and Causes of the Wealth of Nations* illustrates that everyone is a laborer and the author creates a list of workers that the many English Victorians would have felt was really a list of shirkers, parasites and vagabonds, a Catherine Gallagher observes (73) much like the description of the goblin men.

"Cooing all together: / They sounded kind and full of loves (ll. 78-79): this is what the merchant men's sales pitch sounds like. In contrast to the enticing sound of their call is the appearance of the goblins. Ratels are carnivorous and look like a badger. The goblin salesmen consume their clients' capital leaving the customer a dying shell of her former self (l. 277-80) and verbally "badger" her using "hard sell" tactics (the goblin song) until the customer buys their wares; "come buy" is repeated twenty-one times in the poem. The welcoming call (l. 111) to buy is honey-like "purring" (l.108-9), "sugar-baited words" (l. 234) targeted directly at Laura's addiction, but the repeating call turns "shrill" (l. 89).

The repetitive nature of the poem, as in "Evening by evening" (l. 32) indicates the tenacious, unrelenting nature of the merchant men. Selling and buying is an unrelenting cycle that eventually bankrupts all those who participate, the buyers and the sellers, financially and morally. John Stuart Mill in *On Liberty* indicates that people in Victorian English society were being shaped by and for the market society (68). This shaping is true of the goblin men and of Laura and Jeanie in Rossetti's poem. And, as Menke discusses, all growth cycles in Victorian England were reorganized into market ones (114).

Lizzie is the dutiful sister whose efforts to contain Laura's acquisitive proclivity are thwarted by the sales pitch of the goblin men. "'Oh,' cried Lizzie, 'Laura, Laura, / You should not peep at goblin men.' / Lizzie cover'd up her eyes" (ll. 48-50). Rossetti's poetry and prose is full of examples of the morally steadfast who refuse to look at temptation. Weiss discusses the actuality of the bankruptcy in Victorian England and the metaphoric associations with the word during that era. The term "bankruptcy" connoted "the threatened self," "moral and spiritual rebirth," and "social apocalyse" to the English Victorians (Weiss 22). All of these types of metaphoric impoverishment appear in Rossetti's poem. Lines 48 through 50 of *Goblin Market* are Rossetti's statement concerning what Weiss defines as the accommodation between morally threatened self in conflict with public life (88).

How does a moral person maneuver through the maze of temptation in the public world of commerce? The economic identity of an English Victorian was very vulnerable to devastating consequences from which the person would never completely recover. It was not just the loss of money that was at issue; bankruptcy represented a deeper terror, that all the prosperity and optimism of 19th-century was really a sham (88). Bankruptcy was a crisis that caused the individual to lose social position and therefore re-evaluate emotional and religious values and sexual roles; this personal upheaval was more unsettling than the threat of poverty (95). A person like Lizzie with her eyes covered up (ll. 50-51) is shutting out temptation (Laura entices, "Look, Lizzie, look, Lizzie, / Down the glen tramp little men" ll. 54-55) and looking inward to evaluate and re-affirm the identity that the person believes is there. Lizzie is afraid that looking at the goblin men and their wares, looking at the face of consumption, will drain the life out of her, the essence of who she is and what she stands for. And she is correct in this assessment of the situation, as is witnessed by her sister's rapid decline after consuming the goblin merchants' wares (l. 288, 297-8).

Her instincts and memories assist her in maintaining her identity. She warns Laura about another maiden who bought into the merchant men's sales tactics:

> Do you not remember Jeanie,
> How she met them in the moonlight,
> Took their gifts both choice and many,
> Ate their fruits and wore their flowers
> Plucked from bowers
> Where summer ripens at all hours?
> But ever in the noonlight
> She pined and pined away;
> Sought them by night and day,
> Found them no more, but dwindled and grew grey;
> Then fell with the first snow,
> While to this day no grass will grow
> Where she lies low:
> I planted daisies there a year ago
> That never blow. (ll. 147-61).

Jeanie's consumerism was costly; she lost her identity, her morality, her life and more important, her soul, due to her consumer addiction. As Jon Stobart indicates, consumption transforms the consumer; consumer identity is produced and recreated by shopping practices and the act of consumption itself (14). What's more, nothing can grow where Jeanie was buried. Her consumption and the bankruptcy it caused are so polluting that everything is destroyed. Furthermore, in many novels of the English Victorian age, the bankrupt commit suicide, as in Dickens' and Trollope's novels (Weiss 21). Jeanie and Laura commit suicide by continuing to want to "Come buy."

By line 54, all possessiveness and envy have vanished as Laura entices her sister to join her in a shopping spree, validating her "harmless" desire to try out the goblin wares. However, frugal Lizzie will have none of it: "Their evil gifts would harm us" (l. 66). Laura and Lizzie represent the columns in a balance ledger: Laura is the debit side and Lizzie is the credit side. Laura is loss and Lizzie is gain or what they owe versus what they own. Despite Lizzie's warnings, Laura goes to meet the goblin men who are "leering" (l. 93) and "sly" (l. 96) in their first encounter with her, reminiscent of the English Victorian business practices in James Foreman-Peck's research, as well as contemporary used car salesmen. Laura visits them at nighttime, a time when evil transactions occur in fairy tales. Laura stretches to view the bargains (l 81) while the goblins weave her a crude crown of thorns (l. 100). She is a martyr to her shopping frenzy, a sacrifice on the altar of insolvency. But the lure of an exclusive "steal" is too much for Laura's "sweet-tooth" (l. 115): "Men sell not such in any town" (l. 101). The language Rossetti uses is all merchantile:

> "Good folk, I have no coin;
> To take were to purloin:
> I have no copper in my purse,
> I have no silver either,
> And all my gold is on the furze
> That shakes in windy weather
> Above the rusty heather."
> "You have much gold upon your head,"
> They answer'd all together:
> "Buy from us with a golden curl."
> She clipp'd a precious golden lock,
> She dropp'd a tear more rare than pearl. (ll. 116-27).

Laura does not want to steal, but the salesmen have no scruples about stealing from her. "The appearance of unfettered free trade [of the merchant men] only masks the fact that they set the terms of the exchange" (Menke 116). Laura is literally "fleeced" and "clipped" by the merchants. The goblins will take money but they would prefer to take the buyer's life and soul, creating an eternal addiction to their product. Their sinister plan includes wanting the person to buy and then they want the buyer to be so consumed by the product that the buyer will give up life itself to consume again. This is the definition of addiction in selling and buying. The salesmen are consumed just like the buyers. Once the buyer has purchased, the sellers are suddenly not available for further purchase, because they cannot hang around. The "fruit-merchant men" are "brisk" (l. 241); hanging around is a waste of time and money. They want buying desire to eat up the purchaser, but more importantly, they want to find other victims to ensnare. As Simon Humphries illustrates, "the doubleness of the goblin fruit [. . .] is not evil in itself: the things of the world can be offered, and can be consumed, for good or for harm" (398). It is the obsession with selling and with consumption that is deleterious.

Laura gobbles down the fruit over and over again, not understanding "how should it cloy with length of use?" (l. 133). Catherine Gallagher uses the term "somaeconomics" to indicate the emotional and sensual feelings that people attach to buying, not only the desire to buy but also the aftereffects of a spending spree (4). Laura experiences this before and after she eats the fruit; the character's life and feelings are projected on the product of consumption (5).

The salesmen in Victorian England suffered from a corrosive bankruptcy at the heart of their immoral tactics. Upstanding English Victorian businesses did not get any support from the law; moral flexibility had unfortunate results when supplying goods and services for some businessmen. Local authorities tried to regulate exploitative prices on products and services of private enterprise but they were not always successful in keeping businesses free of sleazy practices (Gallagher, Catherine 4). Insider trading ran rampant (Forman-Peck 2); however, by the end of the 1840s, almost all companies were conducting, or had completed, investigations into real or alleged financial irregularities by their officers (2). "In 1895, the Comptroller General for Bankruptcies reported that many liquidations still occurred solely because joint stock companies provided the opportunity to defraud creditors" (3). So, the goblin men's unscrupulous practices are grounded in fact.

Laura heads for home after a consuming frenzy, "And knew not was it night or day" (l. 139). Her buying addiction is disorienting; it puts her in a haze. When Lizzie sees her sister, she is frightened by Laura's stupor and warns her about the bankrupt state that their friend Jeanie got herself into that ultimately killed her. She tries to warn Laura, but Laura's immediate response is that she intends to go bargain hunting the next night again and bring back some "midnight specials" for Lizzie to try (l. 167-8). In lines 184-98, a comparison is given, in a litany of similes, between the two sisters, yet the reader is conscious that bankruptcy and solvency are two-sides of the same coin, so to speak, especially in lines 210-4. A knock-off bag might look the same, but it is not Gucci. One sister has nothing and the other has everything: greed brings hollowness and stability brings abundance, not abundance of purchases or purchase power but abundance of satisfaction. Self-worth is connected to self-discipline.

Nature is in sync, balanced and stable all around the sisters (mirroring the stability and endurance of Lizzie), not disturbing their rest, but Laura's frenzy for fruit, just will not let her alone. Laura cannot hear the call of the goblin men anymore. Their job is done. She is hooked, so they do not have to call to her anymore to entice her to buy. They are now after her sister, the hard sell. They do not care at all what happens to their past clients. Laura cannot sleep and her passion for buying eats her up inside; Laura does not want to owe in her transactions but she ends up feeling cheated as if the merchant men owe her restitution:

> Then sat up in a passionate yearning,
> And gnash'd her teeth for baulk'd desire, and wept
> As if her heart would break.
> Day after day, night after night,
> Laura kept watch in vain
> In sullen silence of exceeding pain.
> She never caught again the goblin cry:
> "Come buy, come buy;" –
> She never spied the goblin men
> Hawking their fruits along the glen:
> But when the non wax'd bright
> Her hair grew thin and grey;
> She dwindled, as the fair full moon doth turn
> To swift decay and burn
> Her fire away. (ll. 266-80)

Marx is *Das Capital* describes the irrational relationships between people and their material desire (qtd in Lindner 53). Solvency is not something that one can hold on to easily but it is priceless if a person can maintain it, whereas all types of bankruptcy (financial, moral, spiritual) grab hold of someone and chokes the life out of them so that everything the person touches goes bad. Laura buries the kernal stone, her one dried up memento of her buying spree, but it never comes to fruition (ll. 281-6). Laura dreams of her next buy but she is like a person dying of thirst seeing a mirage (ll. 289-90).

Getting rich quick is an illusion and obsessive spending leads to only one place – the poor house. Financial ruin is a burden or "yoke" (l. 308). Laura's depression causes her to stop doing her chores that will maintain the financial stability of the farm and instead she "sat down listless in the chimney-nook / And would not eat" (ll. 297-8). Lizzie longs to find a solution for the waning health of her sister, mentally and physically, but fear that she will have to pay too dearly (l. 311) to unscrupulous businessmen to get her sister the help she needs. Lizzie does not want to end up like Laura and like Jeanie:

> She thought of Jeanie in her grave,
> Who should have been a bride;
> But who for joys brides hopes to have
> Fell sick and died
> In her gay prime. (ll. 312-6)

Jeanie is morally and socially bankrupt; she gives her soul to the goblin men instead of to her fiancé in the solemn union of Christian marriage and loses her life because of her imprudent choices.

Lizzie realizes that she must meet the sleazy businessmen face-to-face if she is to save her sister from ruin, so for the first time in her life, she listens to their sales pitch (ll. 327-8). Lizzie serves as the goblin men's economic foil. She takes with her as a bargaining chip a silver coin (l. 324). Money in Victorian England was moving from a solid foundation of land or gold to a mere abstraction of paper (Weiss 19). She will not give away her gold; she represents the stability in land and gold. The word "gold" is mentioned fifteen times in the poem. Laura is even aware of the country "gold standard"; she admits that "all my gold is on the furze" (l. 120), in the land. The gold of a hooked customer and business solvency is juxtaposed to the "true gold" of personal virtue and pride in the land. However, Lizzie will not give away her golden curl as Laura did. Lizzie wants to secure her assets. Lizzie's silver penny represents the devaluing of the gold standard in Victorian England; she tosses this silver penny at the goblins as a way of telling them what their worth is, basically devalued in her estimation of "value." Value for her is in the land, the cows she and Laura milk, the chickens that produce their eggs. Bankruptcy is a loss, a lack of value.

John Ruskin in *Unto This Last* points out that "all true economy is the 'Law of the House'" (113). New Testament parables of debt, silver coins, merchants, pearls (all elements in *Goblin Market*) influenced Ruskin's ideas of political economy in his book, and Rossetti knew Ruskin through her brother, Dante (Menke 120). The goblins laugh and chuckle (l. 329, 334) because they think they have found another sucker to gobble up (l. 335), but they are in for a rude awakening. Lizzie "punks" them. Financial planning and good "sense" win out over the "cents" of indulgence in Christina Rossetti's tale of credit and debt. Lizzie has the credit of goodness on her side in abundance. Angela Leighton discusses that Laura's loss of her coin and curl to the goblin men juxtaposed to Lizzie's unwillingness to part with her coin is significant; the money and the curl represent innocence. Laura loses hers; Lizzie hangs on to hers. Bankruptcy, moral as well as financial, is about corruption, the loss of innocence. Also, the silver penny is associated with "Maundy coins" tossed by royalty to the poor in Easter celebrations in England, as Mendoza discusses (929). The silver penny associates Lizzie with royalty and with authority and the merchant men to those who serve others. "The silver penny, as a commodity, participates in an imagined network of social relations" (Mendoza 930), but the moral of Rossetti's poem is that the social relations that are of most stability and value are those of family. Maundy pennies are only minted for the royal ritual at Easter and are not used as standard currency in commercial exchange (Mendoza 930).

The goblins pull out all the stops just like a salesman who wants to reel in an innocent prospect: "Mopping and mowing / Full of airs and graces" (ll. 336-7) they try to win over Lizzie. "Chattering like magpies" (l.345), they pitch their dog-and-pony show to Lizzie. The goblins are frenzied (in the same state as Laura because she cannot hear the call to buy) because like sharks in the water, they smell blood. They want that sale more than anything. Feasting is something that is associated with those who sell and those who buy. According to Catherine Gallagher, capital is a life form, a grouping of numerous individual persons responding to pain and pleasure stimuli (50). Laura and the goblins resemble Catherine Gallagher's description of "capital." The merchants take great liberties with Lizzie hugging, kissing and squeezing her to get her to succumb (ll. 348-9). Lizzie tosses the silver penny at them (l. 367) and wants to grab the goods and depart, but the merchants want to get as much filthy lucre out of her as they can. They entreat her to stick around: "Nay, take a seat with us, / Honour and eat with us," / They answer'd grinning: / "Our feast is but beginning" (ll. 368-71). They want her to commune with them, to become one with them, as bankrupt as they are. When the merchant men and their victims loll around consuming fruit, they are being non-productive, adding nothing to their credit and accumulating a deficit.

However, Lizzie does not buy in to their scheme. This infuriates the goblin men. She tries to go home and take back her penny, their "fee"
(l. 389). The goblin men call their client derogatory names to shame her into buying (ll. 394-5); they call her proud and uncivil. In lines 396 and 397, the businessmen show their true colors: they become loud and shoot evil looks in her direction. They

become violent towards her, trying to force her to consume their product (ll 399-407), but she will not do it. The threat of financial ruin causes people to do crazy, immoral things. Also, the merchant men's violence punctuates their lack of power in Lizzie's presence, as Mendoza asserts (933). The salesman must sell goods to stay out of debt.

Lizzie's resistance is so steadfast that the goblin men throw her penny back at her and vanish (ll. 437-46). They see that the silver penny is Lizzie's way of devaluing the capitalist marketplace, of their economic community, and they are rejecting her estimation of industrialization's importance. In addition, bankruptcy is vanquished by resistance to overspending. The goblins return the silver penny because Lizzie has refused to keep up her end of the contract (to become addicted to spending by consuming the product). In transactions with the goblins, there is fine print in the contract (basically, all those who consume will be permanently ruined) and Lizzie is aware of this. Lizzie hears her penny jingling in her pocket (l. 452) and the sound is music to her ears (l. 454). The penny is the way she will trick the tricksters. Saving versus spending brings peace and happiness to her, but more importantly, Lizzie feels fearless (l. 460). Lizzie saves her money and saves her sister. Hoarding and thrift rather than consumption beats debt, as Victor Mendoza indicates (920). "Political economy, this science of wealth [. . . is] simultaneously the science of denial, of want, of thrift, of saving," as Karl Marx expostulates (95). Lizzie brings the figurative fruits of her labor back to her sister who consumes them (ll. 468). Laura is afraid that her sister too has been ruined by the goblin men (l. 483). Laura goes through withdrawl for her addiction but eventually Laura is saved by her sister and becomes a believer in familial securities versus financial risk. Laura realizes that "She gorged on bitterness without a name: / Ah! Fool, to choose such a part / Of soul-consuming care!" (ll. 510-2). Lizzie's "Economic Bail Out Plan" for her sister, Laura, succeeds.

Bankruptcy impacts individual personality, family life, social relationships, and the welfare of the community. "Bankruptcy is a symptom of social disintegration, of a world that was losing its sustaining ties of community, stability and order" (Weiss 20). Karl Marx believed that relationships in the 19th century were dominated by monetary gain, alienating the individual from the community and enslaving the individual to merciless economy (qtd in Weiss 19).

Many years have passed at the end of *Goblin Market*. Laura and Lizzie are mothers (l. 546), Laura tells the story of the goblin men to the children (l. 549): "Would talk about the haunted glen, / The wicked, quaint fruit-merchant men, / Their fruits like honey to the throat / But poison in the blood" (ll. 552-5). Financial ruin can poison family bonds, so Laura passes on the message to the children about the ruin of debt and the importance of family bonds in times of crisis: "For there is not friend like a sister" (l. 562). As Menke puts it, "sisterhood manages to shut down the shop" (128). Sisterhood bankrupts the market and the merchants. Laura is Marx's alienated individual who is saved by the community. Marx's theory of "crises" indicated that crisis is a test of the individual's relationship to the economic system (qtd in Weiss 19). Although in most of the English Victorian writings, the adage "Nothing gold can stay" is the rule, in Rossetti's poem gold does stay. The gold of the land and of personal worth and morality wins out over commercialism. Rossetti's poem is about what we "owe," not financially, but specifically what we owe to family and ultimately, to self.

CONCLUSION

There remains a vast area of Christina Rossetti's work that has been left unexcavated by scholars. Her Italian poetry and children's poetry are areas where literary critics should do further interrogation. A contemporary compilation of the entire complete works of Christina Rossetti including her letters, religious poetry, Italian poetry, children's poetry, and prose works is fertile ground for a scholar willing to take on the task of preserving Rossetti's writings in a more current format.

Works Cited

Adelman, Janet. *Suffocating Mothers*. NY: Routledge, 1992. Print.

Akhtar, Navid. "William Morris and Islamic Art." 18 Aug 2009. BBC radio broadcast. Web. www.theearthlyparadise.com/2009/08/william-morris-and-islamic-art.html.

"Amusing World: Rituals of the Dead." 2pp. *Webcrawler*. Web. 2 Oct 2005. www.starknews.blogspot.com/2005/03/rituals-for-dead.html.

Armond, Andrew D. "Limited Knowledge and the Tractarian Doctrine of Reserve in Christina Rossetti's *The Face of the Deep*." *Victorian Poetry* 48.2 (Summer 2010): 219-39. Print.

Arseneau, Mary. "Incarnation and Interpretation: Christina Rossetti, the Oxford Movement, and 'Goblin Market.'" *Victorian Poetry* 31 (Spring 1993): 79-93. Print.

------. *Symbol and Sacrament: The Incarnational Aesthetic of Christina Rossetti*. London: The University of Western Ontario, 1991. Print.

"Bankruptcy in Victorian England – Threat or Myth?" 2pp. *Metacrawler-- VictorianWeb*. Web. 1 Sept 2009.

Battiscombe, Georgina. *Christina Rossetti: A Divided Life*. NY: Holt, Rinehart and Winston, 1981. Print.

Beachy, Robert, Beatrice Craig, and Alastair Owens, eds. *Women, Business and Finance in Nineteenth-Century Europe*. Oxford: Berg, 2006. Print.

Bell, Mackenzie. *Christina Rossetti*. London: Haskell House Publications, Ltd, 1971. Print.

Browning, Elizabeth Barrett. *Aurora Leigh*. Ed. Kerry McSweeney. NY: Oxford UP, 1993. Print.

Bump, Jerome. "Christina Rossetti and the Pre-Raphaelite Brotherhood." Kent 322-45. Print.

Cary, Elisabeth Luther. *The Rossettis: Dante Gabriel and Christina*. NY: Knickerbocker Press, 1900. Print.

Christensen, Matt. "Can I Know it? – Nay: An Alternative Interpretation of Christina Rossetti's *Goblin Market*." 12 pp. *Victorian Web*. Web. 1 Nov 2009.

Crump, R. W., ed. *The Complete Poems of Christina Rossetti*. Baton Rouge:

Louisiana State UP, 1979. Print.

Damrosch, David. *The Longman Anthology: World Literature*. Vol. A: The Ancient World. NY: Longman, 2004. Print.

Davis, Lloyd, ed. *Virginal Sexuality and Textuality in Victorian Literature*. NY: State University of New York Press, 1993. Print.

Finn, Margot C. *The Character of Credit: Person Debt in English Culture 1740-1914*. Cambridge: Cambridge UP, 2003. Print.

Foreman-Peck, James. "Sleaze and the Victorian Businessman." *History Today* 45.8 (Aug 1995). 5-8. Print.

Forget, Christopher Daniel Michael. *Adam and Eve: Ascending to the Godhead (An Analysis of the Fall in John Milton's Paradise Lost)*. Huntington: Marshall UP, 1994. Print.

Franklin, J. Jeffrey. "The Life of Buddha in Victorian England." *ELH* 72.4 (Winter 2005): 941-74. Print.

Gagnier, Regina. "Productive, Reproductive and Consuming Bodies." Horner 43-57. Print.

Gallagher, Catherine. *The Body Economic: Life, Death, and Sensation in Political Economy and the Victorian Novel*. Princeton: Princeton UP, 2006. Print.

Gallagher, Philip J. *Milton, the Bible, and Misogyny*. Columbia: University of Missouri Press, 1990. Print.

Garlick, Barbara. "The Frozen Fountain: Christina Rossetti, the Virgin Model, and Youthful Pre-Raphaelitism." Davis 105-27. Print.

Gibson, Gail McMurray. *The Theater of Devotion. East AnglicanDrama and Society in the Late Middle Ages*. Chicago: University of Chicago Press, 1989. Print.

Gilbert, Sandra M. and Susan Gubar. *The Madwoman in the Attic*. New Haven: Yale UP, 1979. Print.

Gosse, Sir Edmund and Thomas James Wise, eds. *The Complete Works of Swinburne*. NY: Russell and Russell, 1968. Print.

Harrison, Antony H. "Christina Rossetti and the Sage Discourse of Feminist High Anglicanism." *Victorian Sages and Cultural Discourse in Victorian Literature and Art*. Ed. Thais E. Morgan. New Brunswick: Rutgers UP, 1990. 87-104. Print.

------. *Christina Rossetti in Context*. Chapel Hill: North Carolina UP, 1988.

Print.

Harvey, Nancy Lenz. "Margery Kempe: Writer as Creature." *Philological Quarterly* 71 (Spring 1992): 173-84. Print.

Hassett, Constance. *Christina Rossetti: the Patience of Style*. Charlottesville: Virginia UP, 2005. Print.

Helsinger, Elizabeth K. "Consumer Power and the Utopia of Desire: Christina Rossetti's *Goblin Market*." Ed. Joseph Bristow. Victorian Women Poets. NY: St. Martin's Press, 1995. 189-222. Print.

"Hinduism." 1 pag. Reference.com. Webcrawler. Web. 26 Sept 2005. www.reference.com/browse/wiki/Kama.

"Hinduism." 1 pag. *Webcrawler*. Web. 26 Sept 2005. www.religioustolerance.org/hinduism3.htm.

Hobsbawm, Eric. *Industry and Empire: The Birth of the Industrial Revolution*. NY: New Press, 1999. Print.

Holbrook, David. *Images of Women in Literature*. NY: New York UP, 1989. Print.

Holt, Terence. "'Men Sell not Such in any Town': Exchange in *Goblin Market*." *Victorian Poetry* 28.1 (1990): 51-67. Print.

Horner, Avril and Angela Keane, eds. *Body Matters: Feminism, Textuality, Corporeality*. Manchester: Manchester UP, 2000. Print.

Horney, Karen. "The Distrust Between the Sexes." *A World of Ideas*. Ed. Lee A. Jacobus. Boston: Bedford Books of St. Martin's Press, 1994. 317-31. Print.

Humphries, Simon. "The Uncertainty of *Goblin Market*." *Victorian Poetry* 45.4 (2007): 391-413. Print.

Hutcherson, Dudley R. "Milton's Eve and the Other Eves." *Studies in English, Mississippi University* 1 (1960): 12-31. Print.

"Indian Mirror—Culture—Rituals." 1 p. *Webcrawler*. Web. 2 Oct 2005. www.indianmirror.com/culture/cul2.html.

Inglis, R. B., et al. *Adventures in English Literature*. Toronto: W. J. Gage, 1952. 436-7. Print.

Jackson, Leonard. *The Dematerialization of Karl Marx: Literature and Marxist Theory*. London: Longman Group Limited, 1994. Print.

Kay, Alison C. "Retailing, Respectability and the Independent Woman in

Nineteenth-century London." Beachy 152-66. Print.

Kempe, Margery. *The Book of Margery Kempe.* Trans. B.A. Windeatt. NY: Penguin Classics, 1985. Print.

Kent, David A., ed. *The Achievement of Christina Rossetti.* Ithaca: Cornell UP, 1987. Print.

Kooistra, Lorraine Janzen. *Christina Rossetti and Illustration.* Athens: Ohio UP, 2002. Print.

Lash, Jon. "Credit and Debt in Victorian England." 3pp. *Metacrawler.* Web. 1 Sept 2009. www.clas.ufl.edu/users/agunn/teaching.htm.

Leighton, Angela. *Victorian Women Poets: Writing Against the Heart.* Charlottesville: UP of Virginia, 1992. Print.

Lester, V Markham. *Victorian Insolvency: Bankruptcy, Imprisonment for Debt, and Company Winding-Up in Nineteenth-Century England.* Oxford: Oxford UP, 1995. Print.

Lewalski, Barbara K. "Milton on Women - Yet Once More." *Milton Studies* 6 (1975): 3-20. Print.

Lindner, Christoph. *Fictions of Commodity Culture from the Victorian to The Postmodern.* Hampshire: Ashgate Publishing Limited, 2003. Print.

Livingston, James. C. "Tennyson, Jowett, and the Chinese Buddhist Pilgrims." *Victorian Poetry* 27.2 (Summer 1989): 157-68. Print.

LoTempio, David J. *The World of Hope Deferred: Tractarian Elements in the Poetry of Christina Rossetti.* Buffalo: State University College Press, 1994. Print.

Marsh, Jan. *Christina Rossetti: A Writer's Life.* NY: Viking, 1994. Print.

------. "Christina Rossetti's Vocation: The Importance of *Goblin Market*." *VictorianPoetry* 32 (Autumn-Winter 1994): 233-48. Print.

------. *Pre-Raphaelite Women: Images of Femininity.* NY: Harmony Books, 1987. Print.

Marx, Karl. "Economic and Philosophic Manuscripts of 1844." *The Marx-Engels Reader.* Ed. Robert C. Tucker. NY: Norton, 1978. Print.

Mayberry, Katherine J. *Christina Rossetti and the Poetry of Discovery.* Baton Rouge: Louisiana State UP, 1989. Print.

Mendoza, Victor Roman. "'Come Buy': The Crossing of Sexual and Consumer Desire in Christina Rossetti's *Goblin Market*." *ELH* 73

(2006): 913-47. Print.

Menke, Richard. "The Political Economy of Fruit." Ed. Mary Arseneau, Antony H. Harrison, and Lorraine Janzen Kooistra. *The Culture of Christina Rossetti: Female Poetics and Victorian Contexts.* Athens: Ohio UP, 1999. 104-36. Print.

Mill, John Stuart. *On Liberty.* Ed. Alburey Castell. Northbrook: AHM, 1947. Print.

Nelson, James G. *The Sublime Puritan.* Madison: The University of Wisconsin Press, 1963. Print.

Nunokawa, Jeff. *The Afterlife of Property: Domestic Security and the Victorian Novel.* Princeton: Princeton UP, 1994. Print.

Ono, Ayako. *Japonsime in Britian: Whistler, Menpes, Henry, Hornel and Nineteenth-Century Japan.* London: Routledge Curzon, 2003. Print.

O'Reardon, Kristine Ann. *Christina Rossetti's Fallen Women in Poetry.* Tuscaloosa: University of Alabama Press, 1994. Print.

Owens, Alastair. "'Making Some Provision for the Contingencies to which their Sex is Particularly Liable': Women and Investment in Early Nineteenth-Century England." Beachy 20-35. Print.

Patterson, Annabel, ed. *John Milton.* London: Longman Group UK Limited, 1992. Print.

Plowman, Melanie. "As a Poet Speaking from within Female Limitations." 1 p. *Metacrawler.* Web. 7 May 1997. www.stg.brown.edu/.../crossetti/rossetti6.html.

"Punch Magazine." 1 p. Online. *Victorian Web.* 1 Sept 2009. Web. http://www.spartacus.schoolnet.co.uk/Jpunch.htm.

Roe, Dinah. *Christina Rossetti's Faithful Imagination: the Devotional Poetry and Prose.* Basingstoke: Palgrave MacMillan, 2006. Print.

Rossetti, Christina. *Face of the Deep: A Devotional Commentary on the Apocalypse.* London: Society for Promoting Christian Knowledge, 1895. Microfiche: Call #PR1105.L5x, reel 13286.

------. *Goblin Market and Other Poems.* NY: Dover Publications, Inc., 1994. Print.

------. *Letter and Spirit: Notes on the Commandments.* London: Society for Promoting Christian Knowledge, n.d. Print.

------. *Time Flies: A Reading Diary.* Boston: Roberts Brothers, 1886. Microfiche: Call #PR1105.L5x, reel 13249.

Rossetti, William Michael, ed. *The Poetical Works of Christina Georgina Rossetti.* London: MacMillan and Company, Limited, 1904.

Ruskin, John. *Unto This Last. The Works of John Ruskin.* Ed. E. T. Cook and Alexander Wedderburn. London: George Allen, 1912. Print.

Scheinberg, Cynthia. *Miriam's Daughters: Women's Poetry and Religious Identity in Victorian England.* New Brunswick: University of New Jersey Press, 1992. Print.

Schofield, Linda. "Being and Understanding: Devotional Poetry of Christina Rossetti and The Tractarians." Kent 301-21. Print.

Seiken, Layman. *Zen Poems of China and Japan.* Trans. Lucien Stryk, Takashi Ikemoto, And Taigan Takyama. Tokyo, 1973. Print.

Shawcross, John T., ed. *The Complete Poetry of John Milton.* NY: Doubleday, 1971. Print.

------. *John Milton: The Self and the World.* Lexington: University Press of Kentucky, 1993. Print.

Smith, Herbert Augustine, ed. *Macaulay's Essays on Addison and Milton.* Boston: Ginn and Company Publishers, 1902. Print.

Smith, Vickie Jan. *Christina Rossetti's Religious Vision in* <u>Goblin Market</u>. Abilene: Abilene Christian UP, 1992. Print.

Smulders, Sharon. *Christina Rossetti Revisited.* NY: Twayne Publishers, 1996. Print.

Stobart, Jon, Andrew Hann, and Victoria Morgan. *Spaces of Consumption: Leisure and Shopping in the English Town, c. 168-1830.* London: Routledge, 2007. Print.

Stuart, Dorothy Margaret. *Christina Rossetti.* London: Macmillan and Company, Ltd., 1930. Print.

Sullivan, Mary Kathleen. *Milton, Eve, and the Scholars and Critics.* Ann Arbor: University Microfilms International, 1985. Print.

Tennyson, G.B. *Victorian Devotional Poetry: The Tractarian Mode.* Cambridge: Harvard UP, 1981. Print.

Thorpe, James, ed. *Milton Criticism: Selections from Four Centuries.* NY: Rinehart & Company, Inc., 1950. Print.

Weiss, Barbara. *The Hell of the English: Bankruptcy and the Victorian*

Novel. London: Associated University Presses, 1986. Print.

Willbern, David. "Shakespeare's Nothing." *Representing Shakespeare: New Psychoanalytic Essays.* Eds. Murray M. Schwartz and Coppelia Kahn. London: Johns Hopkins UP, 1980. 244-63. Print.

Williams, Thomas Jay and Allan Walter Campbell. *The Park Village Sisterhood.* London: Society for Promoting Christian Knowledge, 1965. Print.

Wittreich, Joseph Anthony. *Feminist Milton.* London: Cornell UP, 1987. Print.

Zonana, Joyce. "The Embodied Muse: Elizabeth Barrett Browning's Aurora Leigh and Feminist Poetics. " *Tulsa Studies in Women's Literature* 2 (1989): 241-62. Print.

Zunder, William and Suzanne Trill, eds. *Writing and the English Renaissance.* NY: Longman Group Limited, 1996. Print.

Works Consulted

Banting, Pamela. "The Body as Pictogram: Rethinking Helene Cixous' *Ecriture Feminine.*" Textual Practice 6 (Summer 1992): 225-46. Print.

Carpenter, Mary Wilson. "'Eat Me, Drink Me, Love Me': The Consumable Female Body in Christina Rossetti's *Goblin Market.*" Cosslett 212-33. Print.

Dante, Alighieri. *Divine Comedy.* Trans. John D. Sinclair. NY: Oxford UP, 1980. Print.

Foucault, Michel. *The Order of Things.* NY: Random House, 1994. Print.

Hankins, James. "Plato's Third Eye: Studies in Marsilio Ficino's Metaphysics and Its Sources." *Renaissance Quarterly* 22 March 1998. Print.

Harrison, Anthony H. "Christina Rossetti: Illness and Ideology." *Victorian Poetry* 45.4 (2007): 415-28. Print.

Hu, Esther T. "Christina Rossetti, John Keble, and the Divine Gaze." *Victorian Poetry* 46.2 (Summer 2008): 175-86. Print.

Maxwell, Catherine. "Tasting the 'Fruit Forbidden': Gender, Intertextuality, And Christina Rossetti's *Goblin Market.*" Ed. Mary Arsenau, Antony H. Harrison, and Lorraine Janzen Kooistra. *The Culture of*

Christina Rossetti: Female Poetics and Victorian Contexts. Athens: Ohio UP, 1999. Print.

Plato. *The Republic*. Trans. G. M. A. Grude and C. D. C. Reeve. NY: Hackett, 1992. Print.

Rosenblum, Dolores. Christina Rossetti's Religious Poetry: Watching, Looking, Keeping Vigil." *Victorian Poetry* 20.1 (Spring 1982): 33-49. Print.

Rossetti, Christina. *Maude*. Ed. Elaine Showalter. *Maude, On Sisterhoods: A Woman's Thoughts About Women*. NY: New York U P, 1993. 3-44. Print.

Waldman, Suzanne. *"The Demon and the Damozel": Dynamics of Desire in the Works of Christina Rossetti and Dante Gabriel Rossetti*. Athens: Ohio UP, 2008. Print.

Webber, Joan Mallory. "The Politics of Poetry: Feminism and *Paradise Lost*." *Milton Studies* (1980): 3-29. Print.

Wiesenthal, Christine. "Regarding Christina Rossetti's 'Reflection.'" *Victorian Poetry* 39.3 (Fall 2001): 389-406. Print.

Wollstonecraft, Mary. *A Vindication of the Rights of Women*. NY: Alfred A. Knopf, Inc., 1992. Print.

APPENDIX I

GOBLIN MARKET

       Morning and evening
       Maids heard the goblins cry:
       "Come buy our orchard fruits,
       Come buy, come buy:
       Apples and quinces,
       Lemons and oranges,
       Plump unpecked cherries,
       Melons and raspberries,
       Bloom-down-cheeked peaches,
       Swart-headed mulberries,
       Wild free-born cranberries,
       Crab-apples, dewberries,
       Pine-apples, blackberries,
       Apricots, strawberries;--
       All ripe together
       In summer weather,--
       Morns that pass by,
       Fair eves that fly;
       Come buy, come buy:
       Our grapes fresh from the vine,
       Pomegranates full and fine,
       Dates and sharp bullaces,
       Rare pears and greengages,
       Damsons and bilberries,
       Taste them and try:
       Currants and gooseberries,
       Bright-fire-like barberries,

Figs to fill your mouth,
Citrons from the South,
Sweet to tongue and sound to eye;
Come buy, come buy."

  Evening by evening
Among the brookside rushes,
Laura bowed her head to hear,
Lizzie veiled her blushes:
Crouching close together
In the cooling weather,
With clasping arms and cautioning lips,
With tingling cheeks and finger tips.
"Lie close," Laura said,
Pricking up her golden head:
"We must not look at goblin men,
We must not buy their fruits:
Who knows upon what soil they fed
Their hungry thirsty roots?"
"Come buy," call the goblins
Hobbling down the glen.
"Oh," cried Lizzie, "Laura, Laura,
You should not peep at goblin men."
Lizzie covered up her eyes,
Covered close lest they should look;
Laura reared her glossy head,
And whispered like the restless brook:
"Look, Lizzie, look, Lizzie,
Down the glen tramp little men.
One hauls a basket,
One bears a plate,
One lugs a golden dish
Of many pounds weight.
How fair the vine must grow
  Whose grapes are so luscious;

How warm the wind must blow
Thro' those fruit bushes."
"No," said Lizzie: "No, no, no;
Their offers should not charm us,
Their evil gifts would harm us."
She thrust a dimpled finger
In each ear, shut eyes and ran:
Curious Laura chose to linger
Wondering at each merchant man.
One had a cat's face,
One whisked a tail,
One tramped at a rat's pace,
One crawled like a snail,
One like a wombat prowled obtuse and furry,
One like a ratel tumbled hurry skurry.
She heard a voice like voice of doves
Cooing all together:
They sounded kind and full of loves
In the pleasant weather.

Laura stretched her gleaming neck
Like a rush-imbedded swan,
Like a lily from the beck,
Like a moonlit poplar branch,
Like a vessel at the launch
When its last restraint is gone.

Backwards up the mossy glen
Turned and trooped the goblin men,
With their shrill repeated cry,
"Come buy, come buy."
When they reached where Laura was
They stood stock still upon the moss,
Leering at each other,

Brother with queer brother;
Signalling each other,
Brother with sly brother.
One set his basket down,
One reared his plate;
One began to weave a crown
Of tendrils, leaves and rough nuts brown
(Men sell not such in any town);
One heaved the golden weight
Of dish and fruit to offer her:
"Come buy, come buy," was still their cry.
Laura stared but did not stir,
Longed but had no money:
The whisk-tailed merchant bade her taste
In tones as smooth as honey,
The cat-faced purr'd,
The rat-paced spoke a word
Of welcome, and the snail-paced even was heard;
One parrot-voiced and jolly
Cried "Pretty Goblin" still for "Pretty Polly;"--
One whistled like a bird.

  But sweet-tooth Laura spoke in haste:
"Good folk, I have no coin;
To take were to purloin:
I have no copper in my purse,
I have no silver either,
And all my gold is on the furze
That shakes in windy weather
Above the rusty heather."
"You have much gold upon you head,"
They answered all together:
"Buy from us with a golden curl."
She clipped a precious golden lock,
She dropped a tear more rare than pearl,

Then sucked their fruit globes fair or red:
Sweeter than honey from the rock,
Stronger than man-rejoicing wine,
Clearer than water flowed that juice;
She never tasted such before,
How should it cloy with length of use?
She sucked and sucked and sucked the more
Fruits which that unknown orchard bore;
She sucked until her lips were sore;
Then flung the emptied rinds away
But gathered up one kernel-stone,
And knew not was it night or day
As she turned home alone.
  Lizzie met her at the gate
Full of wise upbraidings:
"Dear, you should not stay so late,
Twilight is not good for maidens;
Should not loiter in the glen
In the haunts of goblin men.
Do you not remember Jeanie,
How she met them in the moonlight,
Took their gifts both choice and many,
Ate their fruits and wore their flowers
Plucked from bowers
Where summer ripens at all hours?
But ever in the noonlight
She pined and pined away;
Sought them by night and day,
Found them no more, but dwindled and grew grey;
Then fell with the first snow,
While to this day no grass will grow
Where she lies low:
I planted daisies there a year ago
That never blow.

You should not loiter so."
"Nay, hush," said Laura:
"Nay, hush, my sister:
I ate and ate my fill,
Yet my mouth waters still;
To-morrow night I will
Buy more;" and kissed her:
"Have done with sorrow;
I'll bring you plums to-morrow
Fresh on their mother twigs,
Cherries worth getting;
You cannot think what figs
My teeth have met in,
What melons icy-cold
Piled on a dish of gold
Too huge for me to hold,
What peaches with a velvet nap,
Pellucid grapes without one seed:
Odorous indeed must be the mead
Whereon they grow, and pure the wave they drink
With lilies at the brink,
And sugar-sweet their sap."
  Golden head by golden head,
Like two pigeons in one nest
Folded in each other's wings,
They lay down in their curtained bed:
Like two blossoms on one stem,
Like two flakes of new-fall'n snow,
Like two wands of ivory
Tipped with gold for awful kings.
Moon and stars gazed in at them,
Wind sang to them lullaby,
Lumbering owls forbore to fly,
Not a bat flapped to and fro
Round their rest:

Cheek to cheek and breast to breast
Locked together in one nest.

　Early in the morning
When the first cock crowed his warning
Neat like bees, as sweet and busy,
Laura rose with Lizzie:
Fetched in honey, milked the cows,
Aired and set to rights the house,
Kneaded cakes of whitest wheat,
Cakes for dainty mouths to eat,
Next churned butter, whipped up cream,
Fed their poultry, sat and sewed;
Talked as modest maidens should:
Lizzie with an open heart,
Laura in an absent dream,
One content, one sick in part;
One warbling for the mere bright day's delight,
One longing for the night.

　At length slow evening came:
They went with pitchers to the reedy brook;
Lizzie most placid in her look,
Laura most like a leaping flame.
They drew the gurgling water from its deep;
Lizzie plucked purple and rich golden flags,
Then turning homewards said: "The sunset flushes
Those furthest loftiest crags;
Come, Laura, not another maiden lags,
No wilful squirrel wags,
The beasts and birds are fast asleep."
But Laura loitered still among the rushes
And said the bank was steep.

And said the hour was early still,
The dew not fall'n, the wind not chill:
Listening ever, but not catching
The customary cry,
"Come buy, come buy,"
With its iterated jingle
Of sugar-baited words:
Not for all her watching
Once discerning even one goblin
Racing, whisking, tumbling, hobbling;
Let alone the herds
That used to tramp along the glen,
In groups or single,
Of brisk fruit-merchant men.

  Till Lizzie urged, "O Laura, come;
I hear the fruit-call, but I dare not look:
You should not loiter longer at this brook:
Come with me home.
The stars rise, the moon bends her arc,
Each glowworm winks her spark,
Let us get home before the night grows dark:
For clouds may gather
Though this is summer weather,
Put out the lights and drench us through;
Then if we lost our way what should we do?"

  Laura turned cold as stone
To find her sister heard that cry alone,
That goblin cry,
"Come buy our fruits, come buy."
Must she then buy no more such dainty fruit?
Must she no more such succous pasture find,
Gone deaf and blind?
Her tree of life drooped from the root:

She said not one word in her heart's sore ache;
But peering thro' the dimness, nought discerning,
Trudged home, her picher dripping all the way;
So crept to bed, and lay
Silent till Lizzie slept;
Then sat up in a passionate yearning,
And gnashed her teeth for baulked desire, and wept
As if her heart would break.

  Day after day, night after night,
Laura kept watch in vain
In sullen silence of exceeding pain.
She never caught again the goblin cry:
"Come buy, come buy;"--
She never spied the goblin men
Hawking their fruits along the glen:
But when the noon waxed bright
Her hair grew thin and grey;
She dwindled, as the fair full moon doth turn
To swift decay and burn
Her fire away.

  One day remembering her kernel-stone
She set it by a wall that faced the south;
Dewed it with tears, hoped for a root,
Watched for a waxing shoot,
But there came none;
It never saw the sun,
It never felt the trickling moisture run:
While with sunk eyes and faded mouth
She dreamed of melons, as a traveler sees
False waves in desert drouth
With shade of leaf-crowned trees,
And burns the thirstier in the sandful breeze.

She no more swept the house,
Tended the fowls or cows,
Fetched honey, kneaded cakes of wheat,
Brought water from the brook:
But sat down listless in the chimney-nook
And would not eat.

Tender Lizzie could not bear
To watch her sister's cankerous care
Yet not to share.
She night and morning
Caught the goblins' cry:
"Come buy our orchard fruits,
Come buy, come buy:"--
Beside the brook, along the glen,
She heard the tramp of goblin men,
The voice and stir
Poor Laura could not hear;
Longed to buy fruit to comfort her,
But feared to pay too dear.
She thought of Jeanie in her grave,
Who should have been a bride;
But who for joys brides hope to have
Fell sick and died
In her gay prime,
In earliest Winter time,
With the first glazing rime,
With the first snow-fall of crisp Winter time.

Till Laura dwindling
Seemed knocking at Death's door:
Then Lizzie weighed no more
Better and worse;
But put a silver penny in her purse,

Kissed Laura, crossed the heath with clumps of furze
At twilight, halted by the brook:
And for the first time in her life
Began to listen and look.

  Laughed every goblin
When they spied her peeping:
Came towards her hobbling,
Flying, running, leaping,
Puffing and blowing,
Chuckling, clapping, crowing,
Clucking and gobbling,
Mopping and mowing,
Full of airs and graces,
Pulling wry faces,
Demure grimaces,
Cat-like and rat-like,
Ratel- and wombat-like,
Snail-paced in a hurry,
Parrot-voiced and whistler,
Helter skelter, hurry skurry,
Chattering like magpies,
Fluttering like pigeons,
Gliding like fishes,--
Hugged her and kissed her:
Squeezed and caressed her:
Stretched up their dishes,
Panniers, and plates:
"Look at our apples
Russet and dun,
Bob at our cherries,
Bite at our peaches,
Citrons and dates,
Grapes for the asking,

Pears red with basking
Out in the sun,
Plums on their twigs;
Pluck them and suck them,
Pomegranates, figs."--

  "Good folk," said Lizzie,
Mindful of Jeanie:
"Give me much and many:"--
Held out her apron,
Tossed them her penny.
"Nay, take a seat with us,
Honour and eat with us."
They answered grinning:
"Our feast is but beginning,
Night yet is early,
Warm and dew-pearly,
Wakeful and starry:
Such fruits as these
No man can carry;
Half their bloom would fly,
Half their dew would dry,
Half their flavour would pass by.
Sit down and feast with us,
Be welcome guest with us,
Cheer you and rest with us."--
"Thank you," said Lizzie: "But one waits
At home alone for me:
So without further parleying,
If you will not sell me any
Of your fruits though much and many,
Give me back my silver penny
I tossed you for a fee."--
They began to scratch their pates,
No longer wagging, purring,

But visibly demurring,
Grunting and snarling.
One called her proud,
Cross-grained, uncivil;
Their tones waxed loud,
Their looks were evil.
Lashing their tails
They trod and hustled her,
Elbowed and jostled her,
Clawed with their nails,
Barking, mewing, hissing, mocking,
Tore her gown and soiled her stocking,
Twitched her hair out by the roots,
Stamped upon her tender feet,
Held her hands and squeezed their fruits
Against her mouth to make her eat.

  White and golden Lizzie stood,
Like a lily in a flood,--
Like a rock of blue-veined stone
Lashed by tides obstreperously,--
Like a beacon left alone
In a hoary roaring sea,
Sending up a golden fire,--
Like a fruit-crowned orange-tree
White with blossoms honey-sweet
Sore beset by wasp and bee,--
Like a royal virgin town
Topped with gilded dome and spire
Close beleaguered by a fleet
Mad to tug her standard down.

  One may lead a horse to water,
Twenty cannot make him drink.

Though the goblins cuffed and caught her,
Coaxed and fought her,
Bullied and besought her,
Scratched her, pinched her black as ink,
Kicked and knocked her,
Mauled and mocked her,
Lizzie uttered not a word;
Would not open lip from lip
Lest they should cram a mouthful in:
But laughed in heart to feel the drip
Of juice that syrupped all her face,
And lodged in dimples of her chin,
And streaked her neck which quaked like curd.
At last the evil people,
Worn out by her resistance,
Flung back her penny, kicked their fruit
Along whichever road they took,
Not leaving root or stone or shoot;
Some writhed into the ground,
Some dived into the brook
With ring and ripple,
Some scudded on the gale without a sound,
Some vanished in the distance.

  In a smart, ache, tingle,
Lizzie went her way;
Knew not was it night or day;
Sprang up the bank, tore thro' the furze,
Threaded copse and dingle,
And heard her penny jingle
Bouncing in her purse,--
Its bounce was music to her ear.
She ran and ran
As if she feared some goblin man
Dogged her with gibe or curse

Or something worse:
But not one goblin skurried after,
Nor was she pricked by fear;
The kind heart made her windy-paced
That urged her home quite out of breath with haste
And inward laughter.

  She cried "Laura," up the garden,
"Did you miss me?
Come and kiss me.
Never mind my bruises,
Hug me, kiss me, suck my juices
Squeezed from goblin fruits for you,
Goblin pulp and goblin dew.
Eat me, drink me, love me;
Laura, make much of me;
For your sake I have braved the glen
And had to do with goblin merchant men."

  Laura started from her chair,
Flung her arms up in the air,
Clutched her hair:
"Lizzie, Lizzie, have you tasted
For my sake the fruit forbidden?
Must your light like mine be hidden,
Your young life like mine be wasted,
Undone in mine undoing,
And ruined in my ruin,
Thirsty, cankered, goblin-ridden?"--
She clung about her sister,
Kissed and kissed and kissed her:
Tears once again
Refreshed her shrunken eyes,
Dropping like rain

After long sultry drouth;
Shaking with aguish fear, and pain,
She kissed and kissed her with a hungry mouth.

 Her lips began to scorch,
That juice was wormwood to her tongue,
She loathed the feast:
Writhing as one possessed she leaped and sung,
Rent all her robe, and wrung
Her hands in lamentable haste,
And beat her breast.
Her locks streamed like the torch
Borne by a racer at full speed,
Or like the mane of horses in their flight,
Or like an eagle when she stems the light
Straight toward the sun,
Or like a caged thing freed,
Or like a flying flag when armies run.

Swift fire spread through her veins, knocked at
                her heart,
Met the fire smouldering there
And overbore its lesser flame;
She gorged on bitterness without a name:
Ah! fool, to choose such part
Of soul-consuming care!
Sense failed in the mortal strife:
Like the watch-tower of a town
Which an earthquake shatters down,
Like a lightning-stricken mast,
Like a wind-uprooted tree
Spun about,
Like a foam-topped waterspout
Cast down headlong in the sea
She fell at last;

Pleasure past and anguish past,
Is it death or is it life?

  Life out of death,
That night long Lizzie watched by her,
Counted her pulse's flagging stir,
Felt for her breath,
Held water to her lips, and cooled her face
With tears and fanning leaves:
But when the first birds chirped about their eaves,
And early reapers plodded to the place
Of golden sheaves,
And dew-wet grass
Bowed in the morning winds so brisk to pass,
And new buds with new day
Opened of cup-like lilies on the stream,
Laura awoke as from a dream,
Laughed in the innocent old way,
Hugged Lizzie but not twice or thrice;
Her gleaming locks showed not one thread of grey
Her breath was sweet as May
And light danced in her eyes.

  Days, weeks, months, years
Afterwards, when both were wives
With children of their own;
Their mother-hearts beset with fears,
Their lives bound up in tender lives;
Laura would call the little ones
And tell them of her early prime,
Those pleasant days long gone
Of not-returning time:
Would talk about the haunted glen,
The wicked, quaint fruit-merchant men,

Their fruits like honey to the throat
But poison in the blood;
(Men sell not such in any town):
Would tell them how her sister stood
In deadly peril to do her good,
And win the fiery antidote:
Then joining hands to little hands
Would bid them cling together,
"For there is no friend like a sister
In calm or stormy weather;
To cheer one on the tedious way,
To fetch one if one goes astray,
To lift one if one totters down,
To strengthen whilst one stands." (Crump 1, 11-26)

Melanie Ann Hanson
Decapitation and Disgorgement
The Female Body's Text in Early Modern English Drama and Poetry

ISBN 978-3-89821-605-0
180 pages, Paperback. € 24,90

This book brings the ideas of French feminist Hélène Cixous to bear on a number of Early Modern English texts. The female characters of Mariam from Elizabeth Cary's *The Tragedy of Mariam*, Lavinia from William Shakespeare's *Titus Andronicus* as well as John Milton's Eve in *Paradise Lost* and the poetic voice of Isabella Whitney are investigated through the application of Cixous's theories of figurative decapitation and disgorgement. The author examines the creation of a unique discourse through the blending of what is stereotypically referred to as "female text" with "male discourse," which results in what Cixous would call "bisexual discourse."

The author:
Melanie Hanson is at present an Assistant Professor of English at Sam Houston State University. Her publications focus on women writers and women's issues, including her most recent research on contemporary decapitation advertising in Las Vegas, Nevada and the children's novels of Native American author Louise Erdrich. Melanie Hanson's next book will examine adolescent literature written in Victorian England by Bessie Marchant, Emma E. Hornibrook and Jennie Chappell.

Published within the series *Studies in English Literatures*, edited by Koray Melikoğlu.

Please order via fax: +49 511 26 222 01 | by phone: +49 511 26 222 00 | online: www.ibidem-verlag.de
amazon.co.uk

***ibidem*-Verlag**

Melchiorstr. 15

D-70439 Stuttgart

info@ibidem-verlag.de

www.ibidem-verlag.de
www.ibidem.eu
www.edition-noema.de
www.autorenbetreuung.de